THIS BOOK BELONGS TO

_____

_____

START DATE _____ / _____ / _____

HE READS TRUTH

FOUNDERS

FOUNDER
Raechel Myers

CO-FOUNDER
Amanda Bible Williams

EXECUTIVE

CHIEF EXECUTIVE OFFICER
Ryan Myers

CHIEF OPERATING OFFICER
Mark D. Bullard

EDITORIAL

MANAGING EDITOR
Lindsey Jacobi, MDiv

PRODUCTION EDITOR
Hannah Little, MTS

ASSOCIATE EDITOR
Kayla De La Torre, MAT

COPY EDITOR
Becca Owens, MA

CREATIVE

DESIGN MANAGER
Kelsea Allen

DESIGNERS
Savannah Ault
Ashley Phillips

MARKETING

MARKETING DIRECTOR
Whitney Hoffmann

GROWTH MARKETING MANAGERS
Katie Bevels
Blake Showalter

PRODUCT MARKETING MANAGER
Krista Squibb

CONTENT MARKETING STRATEGIST
Tameshia Williams, ThM

MARKETING SPECIALIST
Bailey Majewski

OPERATIONS

OPERATIONS DIRECTOR
Allison Sutton

OPERATIONS MANAGER
Mary Beth Steed

GROUP SALES AND ENGAGEMENT SPECIALIST
Karson Speth

OPERATIONS ASSISTANT
Emily Andrews

SHIPPING

SHIPPING MANAGER
Marian Welch

FULFILLMENT LEAD
Kajsa Matheny

FULFILLMENT SPECIALISTS
Hannah Lamb
Kelsey Simpson

COMMUNITY ENGAGEMENT

COMMUNITY ENGAGEMENT MANAGER
Delaney Coleman

COMMUNITY ENGAGEMENT SPECIALISTS
Cait Baggerman
Katy McKnight
Heather Vollono

CONTRIBUTORS

SPECIAL THANKS
Annie Glover
Lauren Haag

SUBSCRIPTION INQUIRIES
orders@hereadstruth.com

COLOPHON

This book was printed offset in Nashville, Tennessee, on 60# Lynx Opaque Text under the direction of He Reads Truth. Cover is 100# Cougar Opaque with a soft touch lamination.

LIVE BY FAITH
A STUDY OF HEBREWS 11

Here in Hebrews 11 we find fellow saints on whose shoulders we can stand.

There is a great comfort found in someone looking across a table and saying, "I get it. You're not alone." We most often hear those words when we're sharing about something difficult—a deep fear about our children, a concern for a friend, a fight with a spouse, a frustration at work, a sadness we're trying to process. In those moments, our suffering cries out for the encouragement from a "Same here!" or a "Me too!" or an "I went through almost the exact same thing."

Hebrews 11 is one big reminder that we're not alone. The believers to whom this letter was written were face-to-face with unfathomable persecution and opposition against the newly established way of Jesus. They needed every reminder they could find to keep going, they needed to know they weren't alone, and they needed encouragement to look up and see that, at the end of the day, Jesus was and is worth it.

After painting a beautiful picture of Christ's fulfillment of the law and demonstrating how Jesus is better than every forerunner that came before Him, the author of Hebrews showcases the faithful—though also flawed—men and women who endured great trial with the hope of faith motivating, guiding, and guarding them.

They, too, suffered.
They, too, endured.
And they, too, lived by faith in the midst of a wide range of hardship, challenge, loss, and uncertainty.

Our circumstances are not the same as those first and second generation Christians. Yet, our experiences require the same faith to endure life in a fallen world. We too can feel like throwing in the towel, wondering if it's worth it to keep moving forward in faith. But here in Hebrews 11 we find fellow saints on whose shoulders we can stand. As we look at the stories of those who have gone before us, we can chart a throughline of God's faithfulness through their lives. And while our own stories of walking with God are being written, we can trust that we also have that same throughline anchoring us.

In reading Hebrews 11, we are going to slow down and get on our metaphorical hands and knees, crawling through the individual stories mentioned in this chapter so that we can know and stand in awe of the kind of God these people of faith trusted and served. And in doing so, our prayer is that we would find encouragement to keep going in our own imperfect stories. To keep walking and living by faith. Because Jesus is indeed worth it.

THE HE READS TRUTH TEAM

Design on Purpose

Each He Reads Truth resource is thoughtfully and artfully designed to highlight the beauty, goodness, and truth of Scripture in a way that reflects the themes of each curated reading plan.

Our design inspiration for this reading plan was the greatness of God's handiwork, both in who He is and what He builds in His people through faith and endurance. We visually depict this spiritual reality through the photographs of pearls and shells that appear throughout this book.

A pearl develops when a parasite or irritant enters the shell of an oyster or mussel (known as mollusks). As the foreign object agitates the mollusk, the creature produces a protective coating that wraps around the irritant. Layer after layer of this coating forms, and in anywhere from six months to several years, a pearl is formed. This process reminded us of the ways that suffering, though unwanted and painful, can produce beautiful things in and through us as we surrender to God in obedience, allowing Him to build up the faith that we need to endure. The mollusk's shell that encased a pearl during its formation also acts as a protectant against the elements—a reminder of how the Lord sustains us along the way.

This is a long process that requires endurance, but like our faith, it holds significant beauty on the other side.

0123456789

A B C D E F G H I J K L M N
O P Q R S T U V W X Y Z

HOW TO USE THIS BOOK

He Reads Truth is a community of men dedicated to reading the Word of God every day. In this **Live by Faith** reading plan, we will read Hebrews 11, along with complementary passages of Scripture, to understand how the hope of Christ gives believers the faith to endure suffering and hardship.

READ & REFLECT

Your **Live by Faith** book focuses primarily on Scripture, with added features to come alongside your time with God's Word.

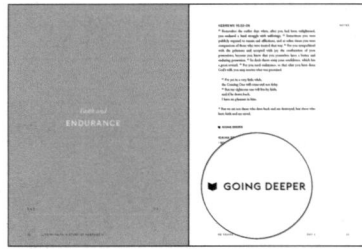

SCRIPTURE READING

Designed for a Monday start, this book presents daily readings from Hebrews 11 and the connected narratives to understand faith through the stories in the chapter.

Additional passages are marked in your daily reading with the Going Deeper heading.

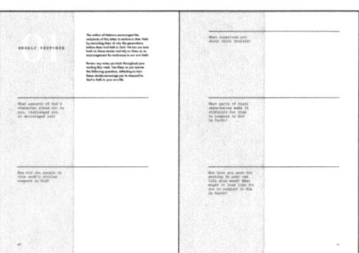

REFLECTION QUESTIONS

Each week features questions and space for personal reflection.

COMMUNITY & CONVERSATION

You can start reading this book at any time. If you want to join men from across the globe as they read along with you, the He Reads Truth community will start Day 1 of **Live by Faith** on Monday, October 14, 2024.

GRACE DAY

Use Saturdays to catch up on your reading, pray, and rest in the presence of the Lord.

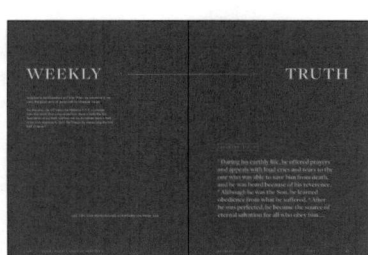

WEEKLY TRUTH

Sundays are set aside for Scripture memorization.

See tips for memorizing Scripture on page 164.

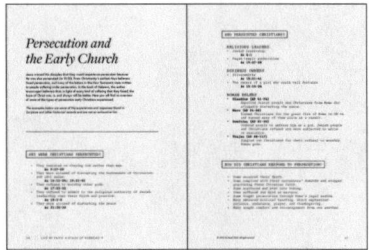

EXTRAS

This book features additional tools to help you gain a deeper understanding of the text.

Find a complete list of extras on page 11.

HE READS TRUTH APP

For added community and conversation, join us in the **Live by Faith** reading plan on the He Reads Truth app. You can use the app to participate in community discussion and more.

HEREADSTRUTH.COM

The **Live by Faith** reading plan and community discussion will also be available at HeReadsTruth.com as the community reads each day. Invite your family, friends, and neighbors to read along with you.

TABLE OF CONTENTS

Now faith is the reality of
what is hoped for, the proof
of what is not seen.

HEBREWS 11:1

Introduction

The Book of Hebrews

The book of Hebrews is a reminder of the worthiness of the gospel in the face of immense suffering. Written to believers who were experiencing great persecution (Heb 10:32-33), Hebrews encourages perseverance and faithfulness despite the temptation to turn away. In chapters 1-10, the author uses the Greek word *kreitton*, which means "more excellent," to recall all the ways Christ is the ultimate fulfillment of the Old Testament's promises and prophecies. Hebrews ties Old Testament history and practices to the life and ministry of Jesus more than any other book in the New Testament, reminding believers of His new and better covenant established by His full and finished work.

Faith in Suffering

The Greek word *pistis*, translated as "faith," means conviction of the truth. For the Christ follower, faith is the persistent trust in God's truth—in Jesus Himself. But when circumstances or seasons in our life cause pain, hardship, or suffering, we can feel unsteady. One of the ways we can have faith in those moments is by looking at the stories of people who have gone before us and seeing how God moved in their circumstances.

In these examples, God builds up a kind of faith that can withstand—a faith that is anchored in both who He is and the hope of His promises. While the people mentioned in Hebrews 11 died without seeing Jesus as the fulfillment of God's promises, we have His life, death, and resurrection as the firm foundation of our hope. We long to see God's promise fully completed in Jesus's return, and yet we know what the people of Hebrews 11 did not—God's Son is the fulfillment of every promise.

We are faithful when we think, hope, and act with that persistent trust in Jesus as our foundation and our guide.

In This Reading Plan

We will read the entirety of Hebrews 11 on Day 1 to see the big picture of faith the author is presenting. Then, on Day 2, we'll go back to Hebrews 10 to see how the author set up chapter 11 as a collection of examples of "those who have faith and are saved" (Heb 10:39) in the middle of many kinds of suffering.

The reading days that follow will take us through those individual stories highlighted in Hebrews 11, further highlighting why God is worthy of our trust, how Christ is our hope in the middle of suffering, and the different ways we can respond to God in faith.

On the last day of the reading plan we'll read Hebrews 11 again, seeing how all of these individual stories weave together to show us a picture of a faith that is fully anchored in who God is. At the end of each week, you'll have space to reflect on how these stories can help shape your own faith.

Live by

FAITH

Today, read Hebrews 11 in its
entirety before turning to the
specific examples of faith on
Days 4 through 31.

HEBREWS 11

LIVING BY FAITH

¹ Now faith is the reality of what is hoped for, the proof of what is not seen. ² For by this our ancestors were approved.

³ By faith we understand that the universe was created by the word of God, so that what is seen was made from things that are not visible.

⁴ By faith Abel offered to God a better sacrifice than Cain did. By faith he was approved as a righteous man, because God approved his gifts, and even though he is dead, he still speaks through his faith.

⁵ By faith Enoch was taken away, and so he did not experience death. He was not to be found because God took him away. For before he was taken away, he was approved as one who pleased God. ⁶ Now without faith it is impossible to please God, since the one who draws near to him must believe that he exists and that he rewards those who seek him.

⁷ By faith Noah, after he was warned about what was not yet seen and motivated by godly fear, built an ark to deliver his family. By faith he condemned the world and became an heir of the righteousness that comes by faith.

⁸ By faith Abraham, when he was called, obeyed and set out for a place that he was going to receive as an inheritance. He went out, even though he did not know where he was going. ⁹ By faith he stayed as a foreigner in the land of promise, living in tents as did Isaac and Jacob, coheirs of the same promise. ¹⁰ For he was looking forward to the city that has foundations, whose architect and builder is God.

¹¹ By faith even Sarah herself, when she was unable to have children, received power to conceive offspring, even though she was past the age, since she considered that the one who had promised was faithful. ¹² Therefore, from one man—in fact, from one as good as dead—came offspring as numerous as the stars of the sky and as innumerable as the grains of sand along the seashore.

¹³ These all died in faith, although they had not received the things that were promised. But they saw them from a distance, greeted them, and confessed that they were foreigners and temporary residents on the earth. ¹⁴ Now those who say such things make it clear that they are seeking a

homeland. ¹⁵ If they were thinking about where they came from, they would have had an opportunity to return. ¹⁶ But they now desire a better place—a heavenly one. Therefore, God is not ashamed to be called their God, for he has prepared a city for them.

¹⁷ By faith Abraham, when he was tested, offered up Isaac. He received the promises and yet he was offering his one and only son, ¹⁸ the one to whom it had been said, Your offspring will be traced through Isaac. ¹⁹ He considered God to be able even to raise someone from the dead; therefore, he received him back, figuratively speaking.

²⁰ By faith Isaac blessed Jacob and Esau concerning things to come. ²¹ By faith Jacob, when he was dying, blessed each of the sons of Joseph, and he worshiped, leaning on the top of his staff. ²² By faith Joseph, as he was nearing the end of his life, mentioned the exodus of the Israelites and gave instructions concerning his bones.

²³ By faith Moses, after he was born, was hidden by his parents for three months, because they saw that the child was beautiful, and they didn't fear the king's edict. ²⁴ By faith Moses, when he had grown up, refused to be called the son of Pharaoh's daughter ²⁵ and chose to suffer with the people of God rather than to enjoy the fleeting pleasure of sin. ²⁶ For he considered reproach for the sake of Christ to be greater wealth than the treasures of Egypt, since he was looking ahead to the reward.

²⁷ By faith he left Egypt behind, not being afraid of the king's anger, for Moses persevered as one who sees him who is invisible. ²⁸ By faith he instituted the Passover and the sprinkling of the blood, so that the destroyer of the firstborn might not touch the Israelites. ²⁹ By faith they crossed the Red Sea as though they were on dry land. When the Egyptians attempted to do this, they were drowned.

³⁰ By faith the walls of Jericho fell down after being marched around by the Israelites for seven days. ³¹ By faith Rahab the prostitute welcomed the spies in peace and didn't perish with those who disobeyed.

³² And what more can I say? Time is too short for me to tell about Gideon, Barak, Samson, Jephthah, David, Samuel, and the prophets, ³³ who by faith conquered kingdoms, administered justice, obtained promises, shut the mouths of lions, ³⁴ quenched the raging of fire, escaped the edge of the sword, gained strength in weakness, became mighty in battle, and

put foreign armies to flight. [35] Women received their dead, raised to life again. Other people were tortured, not accepting release, so that they might gain a better resurrection. [36] Others experienced mockings and scourgings, as well as bonds and imprisonment. [37] They were stoned, they were sawed in two, they died by the sword, they wandered about in sheepskins, in goatskins, destitute, afflicted, and mistreated. [38] The world was not worthy of them. They wandered in deserts and on mountains, hiding in caves and holes in the ground.

[39] All these were approved through their faith, but they did not receive what was promised, [40] since God had provided something better for us, so that they would not be made perfect without us.

Faith and

ENDURANCE

³² Remember the earlier days when, after you had been enlightened, you endured a hard struggle with sufferings. ³³ Sometimes you were publicly exposed to taunts and afflictions, and at other times you were companions of those who were treated that way. ³⁴ For you sympathized with the prisoners and accepted with joy the confiscation of your possessions, because you know that you yourselves have a better and enduring possession. ³⁵ So don't throw away your confidence, which has a great reward. ³⁶ For you need endurance, so that after you have done God's will, you may receive what was promised.

³⁷ For yet in a very little while,
the Coming One will come and not delay.
³⁸ But my righteous one will live by faith;
and if he draws back,
I have no pleasure in him.

³⁹ But we are not those who draw back and are destroyed, but those who have faith and are saved.

GOING DEEPER

ISAIAH 53

¹ Who has believed what we have heard?
And to whom has the arm of the LORD been revealed?
² He grew up before him like a young plant
and like a root out of dry ground.
He didn't have an impressive form
or majesty that we should look at him,
no appearance that we should desire him.
³ He was despised and rejected by men,
a man of suffering who knew what sickness was.
He was like someone people turned away from;
he was despised, and we didn't value him.

⁴ Yet he himself bore our sicknesses,
and he carried our pains;
but we in turn regarded him stricken,
struck down by God, and afflicted.

⁵ But he was pierced because of our rebellion,
crushed because of our iniquities;
punishment for our peace was on him,
and we are healed by his wounds.
⁶ We all went astray like sheep;
we all have turned to our own way;
and the LORD has punished him
for the iniquity of us all.

⁷ He was oppressed and afflicted,
yet he did not open his mouth.
Like a lamb led to the slaughter
and like a sheep silent before her shearers,
he did not open his mouth.
⁸ He was taken away because of oppression and judgment,
and who considered his fate?
For he was cut off from the land of the living;
he was struck because of my people's rebellion.
⁹ He was assigned a grave with the wicked,
but he was with a rich man at his death,
because he had done no violence
and had not spoken deceitfully.

¹⁰ Yet the LORD was pleased to crush him severely.
When you make him a guilt offering,
he will see his seed, he will prolong his days,
and by his hand, the LORD's pleasure will be accomplished.
¹¹ After his anguish,
he will see light and be satisfied.
By his knowledge,
my righteous servant will justify many,
and he will carry their iniquities.
¹² Therefore I will give him the many as a portion,
and he will receive the mighty as spoil,
because he willingly submitted to death,
and was counted among the rebels;

yet he bore the sin of many
and interceded for the rebels.

HEBREWS 5:7–10

[7] During his earthly life, he offered prayers and appeals with loud cries and tears to the one who was able to save him from death, and he was heard because of his reverence. [8] Although he was the Son, he learned obedience from what he suffered. [9] After he was perfected, he became the source of eternal salvation for all who obey him, [10] and he was declared by God a high priest according to the order of Melchizedek.

PHILIPPIANS 3:7–14

[7] But everything that was a gain to me, I have considered to be a loss because of Christ. [8] More than that, I also consider everything to be a loss in view of the surpassing value of knowing Christ Jesus my Lord. Because of him I have suffered the loss of all things and consider them as dung, so that I may gain Christ [9] and be found in him,

not having a righteousness of my own from the law, but one that is through faith in Christ—the righteousness from God based on faith.

[10] My goal is to know him and the power of his resurrection and the fellowship of his sufferings, being conformed to his death, [11] assuming that I will somehow reach the resurrection from among the dead.

REACHING FORWARD TO GOD'S GOAL

[12] Not that I have already reached the goal or am already perfect, but I make every effort to take hold of it because I also have been taken hold of by Christ Jesus. [13] Brothers and sisters, I do not consider myself to have taken hold of it. But one thing I do: Forgetting what is behind and reaching forward to what is ahead, [14] I pursue as my goal the prize promised by God's heavenly call in Christ Jesus.

Persecution and the Early Church

Jesus warned His disciples that they would experience persecution because He was also persecuted (Jn 15:20). From Christianity's earliest days believers faced persecution, and many of the letters in the New Testament were written to people suffering under persecution. In the book of Hebrews, the author encouraged believers that, in light of every kind of suffering that they faced, the hope of Christ was, is, and always will be better. Here you will find an overview of some of the types of persecution early Christians experienced.

The examples here are some of the experiences and responses found in Scripture and other historical records and are not an exhaustive list.

WHY WERE CHRISTIANS PERSECUTED?

- They insisted on obeying God rather than man.
    Ac 5:17-29
- They were accused of disrupting the businesses of divination and idol sales.
    Ac 16:11-24; 19:21-41
- They refused to worship other gods.
    Ac 17:22-32
- They refused to submit to the religious authority of Jewish leadership over their faith and practice.
    Ac 18:1-6
- They were accused of disturbing the peace.
    Ac 21:26-30

WHO PERSECUTED CHRISTIANS?

RELIGIOUS LEADERS
- Jewish leadership
    - **Ac 4:1**
- Pagan temple authorities
    - **Ac 19:27-28**

BUSINESS OWNERS
- Silversmiths
    - **Ac 19:21-41**
- The owners of a girl who could tell fortunes
    - **Ac 16:16-24**

ROMAN RULERS
- **Claudius (AD 41-54)**
    - Expelled Jewish people and Christians from Rome for allegedly disturbing the peace.
- **Nero (AD 54-68)**
    - Blamed Christians for the great fire of Rome in AD 64 and burned many of them alive as a result.
- **Domitian (AD 81-96)**
    - Ordered people to address him as a god. Jewish people and Christians refused and were subjected to exile or execution.
- **Trajan (AD 98-117)**
    - Singled out Christians for their refusal to worship Roman gods.

HOW DID CHRISTIANS RESPOND TO PERSECUTION?

- Some recanted their faith.
- Some complied with their oppressors' demands and stopped practicing their Christian faith.
- Some scattered and went into hiding.
- Some suffered and died as martyrs.
- Some fought persecution through Rome's legal system.
- Many embraced biblical teaching, which emphasized patience, endurance, prayer, and thanksgiving.
- Many sought comfort and encouragement from one another.

The Nature

OF FAITH

Now faith is the reality of what is hoped for, the proof of what is not seen. For by this our ancestors were approved.

HEBREWS 11:1–2

⬤ GOING DEEPER

JOHN 20

THE EMPTY TOMB

¹ On the first day of the week Mary Magdalene came to the tomb early, while it was still dark. She saw that the stone had been removed from the tomb. ² So she went running to Simon Peter and to the other disciple, the one Jesus loved, and said to them, "They've taken the Lord out of the tomb, and we don't know where they've put him!"

³ At that, Peter and the other disciple went out, heading for the tomb. ⁴ The two were running together, but the other disciple outran Peter and got to the tomb first. ⁵ Stooping down, he saw the linen cloths lying there, but he did not go in. ⁶ Then, following him, Simon Peter also came. He entered the tomb and

saw the linen cloths lying there. [7] The wrapping that had been on his head was not lying with the linen cloths but was folded up in a separate place by itself. [8] The other disciple, who had reached the tomb first, then also went in, saw, and believed. [9] For they did not yet understand the Scripture that he must rise from the dead. [10] Then the disciples returned to the place where they were staying.

MARY MAGDALENE SEES THE RISEN LORD

[11] But Mary stood outside the tomb, crying. As she was crying, she stooped to look into the tomb. [12] She saw two angels in white sitting where Jesus's body had been lying, one at the head and the other at the feet. [13] They said to her, "Woman, why are you crying?"

"Because they've taken away my Lord," she told them, "and I don't know where they've put him."

[14] Having said this, she turned around and saw Jesus standing there, but she did not know it was Jesus. [15] "Woman," Jesus said to her, "why are you crying? Who is it that you're seeking?"

Supposing he was the gardener, she replied, "Sir, if you've carried him away, tell me where you've put him, and I will take him away."

[16] Jesus said to her, "Mary."

Turning around, she said to him in Aramaic, *"Rabboni!"*—which means "Teacher."

[17] "Don't cling to me," Jesus told her, "since I have not yet ascended to the Father. But go to my brothers and tell them that I am ascending to my Father and your Father, to my God and your God."

[18] Mary Magdalene went and announced to the disciples, "I have seen the Lord!" And she told them what he had said to her.

THE DISCIPLES COMMISSIONED

[19] When it was evening on that first day of the week, the disciples were gathered together with the doors locked because they feared the Jews. Jesus came, stood among them, and said to them, "Peace be with you."

[20] Having said this, he showed them his hands and his side. So the disciples rejoiced when they saw the Lord.

[21] Jesus said to them again, "Peace be with you. As the Father has sent me, I also send you." [22] After saying this, he breathed on them and said, "Receive the Holy Spirit. [23] If you forgive the sins of any, they are forgiven them; if you retain the sins of any, they are retained."

THOMAS SEES AND BELIEVES

[24] But Thomas (called "Twin"), one of the Twelve, was not with them when Jesus came. [25] So the other disciples were telling him, "We've seen the Lord!"

But he said to them, "If I don't see the mark of the nails in his hands, put my finger into the mark of the nails, and put my hand into his side, I will never believe."

[26] A week later his disciples were indoors again, and Thomas was with them. Even though the

doors were locked, Jesus came and stood among them and said, "Peace be with you."

[27] Then he said to Thomas, "Put your finger here and look at my hands. Reach out your hand and put it into my side. Don't be faithless, but believe."

[28] Thomas responded to him, "My Lord and my God!"

[29] Jesus said, "Because you have seen me, you have believed. Blessed are those who have not seen and yet believe."

THE PURPOSE OF THIS GOSPEL

[30] Jesus performed many other signs in the presence of his disciples that are not written in this book. [31] But these are written so that you may believe that Jesus is the Messiah, the Son of God, and that by believing you may have life in his name.

ACTS 1:6–11

[6] So when they had come together, they asked him, "Lord, are you restoring the kingdom to Israel at this time?"

[7] He said to them, "It is not for you to know times or periods that the Father has set by his own authority. [8] But you will receive power when the Holy Spirit has come on you, and you will be my witnesses in Jerusalem, in all Judea and Samaria, and to the ends of the earth."

THE ASCENSION

[9] After he had said this, he was taken up as they were watching, and a cloud took him out of their sight. [10] While he was going, they were gazing into heaven, and suddenly two men in white clothes stood by them. [11] They said, "Men of Galilee, why do you stand looking up into heaven?

This same Jesus, who has been taken from you into heaven, will come in the same way that you have seen him going into heaven."

By Faith

WE UNDERSTAND

By faith we understand that the universe was
created by the word of God, so that what is seen
was made from things that are not visible.

HEBREWS 11:3

DAY   0 4

GENESIS 1

THE CREATION

¹ In the beginning God created the heavens and the earth.

² Now the earth was formless and empty, darkness covered the surface of the watery depths, and the Spirit of God was hovering over the surface of the waters. ³ Then God said, "Let there be light," and there was light. ⁴ God saw that the light was good, and God separated the light from the darkness. ⁵ God called the light "day," and the darkness he called "night." There was an evening, and there was a morning: one day.

⁶ Then God said, "Let there be an expanse between the waters, separating water from water." ⁷ So God made the expanse and separated the water under the expanse from the water above the expanse. And it was so. ⁸ God called the expanse "sky." Evening came and then morning: the second day.

⁹ Then God said, "Let the water under the sky be gathered into one place, and let the dry land appear." And it was so. ¹⁰ God called the dry land "earth," and the gathering of the water he called "seas." And God saw that it was good. ¹¹ Then God said, "Let the earth produce vegetation: seed-bearing plants and fruit trees on the earth bearing fruit with seed in it according to their kinds." And it was so. ¹² The earth produced vegetation: seed-bearing plants according to their kinds and trees bearing fruit with seed in it according to their kinds. And God saw that it was good. ¹³ Evening came and then morning: the third day.

¹⁴ Then God said, "Let there be lights in the expanse of the sky to separate the day from the night. They will serve as signs for seasons and for days and years. ¹⁵ They will be lights in the expanse of the sky to provide light on the earth." And it was so. ¹⁶ God made the

two great lights—the greater light to rule over the day and the lesser light to rule over the night—as well as the stars. ¹⁷ God placed them in the expanse of the sky to provide light on the earth, ¹⁸ to rule the day and the night, and to separate light from darkness. And God saw that it was good. ¹⁹ Evening came and then morning: the fourth day.

²⁰ Then God said, "Let the water swarm with living creatures, and let birds fly above the earth across the expanse of the sky." ²¹ So God created the large sea-creatures and every living creature that moves and swarms in the water, according to their kinds. He also created every winged creature according to its kind. And God saw that it was good. ²² God blessed them: "Be fruitful, multiply, and fill the waters of the seas, and let the birds multiply on the earth." ²³ Evening came and then morning: the fifth day.

²⁴ Then God said, "Let the earth produce living creatures according to their kinds: livestock, creatures that crawl, and the wildlife of the earth according to their kinds." And it was so. ²⁵ So God made the wildlife of the earth according to their kinds, the livestock according to their kinds, and all the creatures that crawl on the ground according to their kinds. And God saw that it was good.

²⁶ Then God said, "Let us make man in our image, according to our likeness. They will rule the fish of the sea, the birds of the sky, the livestock, the whole earth, and the creatures that crawl on the earth."

²⁷ So God created man
in his own image;
he created him in the image of God;
he created them male and female.

²⁸ God blessed them, and God said to them, "Be fruitful, multiply, fill the earth, and subdue it. Rule the fish of the sea, the birds of the sky, and every creature that crawls on the earth." ²⁹ God also said, "Look, I have given you every seed-bearing plant on the surface of the entire earth and every tree whose fruit contains seed. This will be food for you, ³⁰ for all the wildlife of the earth, for every bird of the sky, and for every creature that crawls on the earth—everything having the breath of life in it—I

As you read the "by faith" statements from Hebrews 11 over the next several weeks, use the space in the margins to make note of how you see God's presence in each story or any reflections on how each person responded to God and expressed their faith in Him.

have given every green plant for food." And it was so. [31] God saw all that he had made, and it was very good indeed. Evening came and then morning: the sixth day.

◖ GOING DEEPER

JOHN 1:1-5

PROLOGUE

[1] In the beginning was the Word, and the Word was with God, and the Word was God. [2] He was with God in the beginning. [3] All things were created through him, and apart from him not one thing was created that has been created. [4] In him was life, and that life was the light of men. [5] That light shines in the darkness, and yet the darkness did not overcome it.

COLOSSIANS 1:15-23

THE CENTRALITY OF CHRIST

[15] He is the image of the invisible God,
the firstborn over all creation.

*[16] For everything was created by him,
in heaven and on earth,
the visible and the invisible,*

whether thrones or dominions
or rulers or authorities—
all things have been created through him and for him.
[17] He is before all things,
and by him all things hold together.
[18] He is also the head of the body, the church;
he is the beginning,
the firstborn from the dead,
so that he might come to have
first place in everything.
[19] For God was pleased to have
all his fullness dwell in him,
[20] and through him to reconcile

everything to himself,
whether things on earth or things in heaven,
by making peace
through his blood, shed on the cross.

[21] Once you were alienated and hostile in your minds as expressed in your evil actions. [22] But now he has reconciled you by his physical body through his death, to present you holy, faultless, and blameless before him— [23] if indeed you remain grounded and steadfast in the faith and are not shifted away from the hope of the gospel that you heard. This gospel has been proclaimed in all creation under heaven, and I, Paul, have become a servant of it.

2 CORINTHIANS 4:6

For God who said, "Let light shine out of darkness," has shone in our hearts to give the light of the knowledge of God's glory in the face of Jesus Christ.

By Faith

ABEL
OFFERED

DAY 05

By faith Abel offered to God a better sacrifice than Cain did. By faith he was approved as a righteous man, because God approved his gifts, and even though he is dead, he still speaks through his faith.

HEBREWS 11:4

GENESIS 4:1-11

CAIN MURDERS ABEL

¹ The man was intimate with his wife Eve, and she conceived and gave birth to Cain. She said, "I have had a male child with the LORD's help." ² She also gave birth to his brother Abel. Now Abel became a shepherd of flocks, but Cain worked the ground. ³ In the course of time Cain presented some of the land's produce as an offering to the LORD. ⁴ And Abel also presented an offering—some of the firstborn of his flock and their fat portions. The LORD had regard for Abel and his offering, ⁵ but he did not have regard for Cain and his offering. Cain was furious, and he looked despondent.

⁶ Then the LORD said to Cain, "Why are you furious? And why do you look despondent? ⁷ If you do what is right, won't you be accepted? But if you do not do what is right, sin is crouching at the door. Its desire is for you, but you must rule over it."

⁸ Cain said to his brother Abel, "Let's go out to the field." And while they were in the field, Cain attacked his brother Abel and killed him.

⁹ Then the LORD said to Cain, "Where is your brother Abel?"

"I don't know," he replied. "Am I my brother's guardian?"

¹⁰ Then he said, "What have you done? Your brother's blood cries out to me from the ground! ¹¹ So now you are cursed, alienated from the ground that opened its mouth to receive your brother's blood you have shed."

ROMANS 10:6-10

[6] But the righteousness that comes from faith speaks like this: Do not say in your heart, "Who will go up to heaven?" that is, to bring Christ down [7] or, "Who will go down into the abyss?" that is, to bring Christ up from the dead. [8] On the contrary, what does it say? The message is near you, in your mouth and in your heart. This is the message of faith that we proclaim: [9] If you confess with your mouth, "Jesus is Lord," and believe in your heart that God raised him from the dead, you will be saved. [10] One believes with the heart, resulting in righteousness, and one confesses with the mouth, resulting in salvation.

1 JOHN 3:11-24

LOVE IN ACTION

[11] For this is the message you have heard from the beginning: We should love one another, [12] unlike Cain, who was of the evil one and murdered his brother. And why did he murder him? Because his deeds were evil, and his brother's were righteous.

[13] Do not be surprised, brothers and sisters, if the world hates you. [14] We know that we have passed from death to life because we love our brothers and sisters. The one who does not love remains in death. [15] Everyone who hates his brother or sister is a murderer, and you know that no murderer has eternal life residing in him. [16] This is how we have come to know love: He laid down his life for us. We should also lay down our lives for our brothers and sisters. [17] If anyone has this world's goods and sees a fellow believer in need but withholds compassion from him—how does God's love reside in him? [18] Little children, let us not love in word or speech, but in action and in truth.

[19] This is how we will know that we belong to the truth and will reassure our hearts before him [20] whenever our hearts condemn us; for God is greater than our hearts, and he knows all things.

[21] Dear friends, if our hearts don't condemn us, we have confidence before God [22] and receive whatever we ask from him because we keep his commands and do what is pleasing in his sight. [23] Now this is his command: that we believe in the name of his Son, Jesus Christ, and love one another as he commanded us. [24] The one who keeps his commands remains in him, and he in him. And the way we know that he remains in us is from the Spirit he has given us.

01

WEEKLY RESPONSE

The author of Hebrews encouraged the recipients of this letter to endure in their faith by reminding them of why the generations before them had faith in God. We too can look back on these stories and rely on them as an encouragement for endurance in our own faith.

Review any notes you took throughout your reading this week. Use them as you answer the following questions, reflecting on how these stories encourage you to respond to God in faith in your own life.

What aspects of God's character stood out to you, challenged you, or encouraged you?

How did the people in this week's stories respond to God?

What surprised you
about their stories?

What parts of their
experiences made it
difficult for them
to respond to God
in faith?

How have you seen God
working in your own
life this week? What
might it look like for
you to respond to Him
in faith?

GRACE DAY

Take this day to catch up on your reading, pray, and rest in the presence of the Lord.

Jesus said, "Because you have seen me, you have believed. Blessed are those who have not seen and yet believe."

JOHN 20:29

WEEKLY

Scripture is God-breathed and true. When we memorize it, we carry the good news of Jesus with us wherever we go.

For this plan, we will memorize Hebrews 5:7–9, a passage from this study that summarizes how Jesus is both the firm foundation of our faith and how we are to imitate Jesus's faith in our own response to God. We'll begin by memorizing the first half of verse 7.

SEE TIPS FOR MEMORIZING SCRIPTURE ON PAGE 164.

TRUTH

[7] During his earthly life, he offered prayers and appeals with loud cries and tears to the one who was able to save him from death, and he was heard because of his reverence. [8] Although he was the Son, he learned obedience from what he suffered. [9] After he was perfected, he became the source of eternal salvation for all who obey him…

By Faith

ENOCH WAS
TAKEN AWAY

By faith Enoch was taken away, and so he did not experience death. He was not to be found because God took him away. For before he was taken away, he was approved as one who pleased God. Now without faith it is impossible to please God, since the one who draws near to him must believe that he exists and that he rewards those who seek him.

HEBREWS 11:5–6

DAY

08

GENESIS 5:21-24

²¹ Enoch was 65 years old when he fathered Methuselah. ²² And after he fathered Methuselah, Enoch walked with God 300 years and fathered other sons and daughters. ²³ So Enoch's life lasted 365 years. ²⁴ Enoch walked with God; then he was not there because God took him.

❤ GOING DEEPER

PSALM 24:1-6

THE KING OF GLORY

A psalm of David.

¹ The earth and everything in it,
the world and its inhabitants,
belong to the LORD;
² for he laid its foundation on the seas
and established it on the rivers.

³ Who may ascend the mountain of the LORD?
Who may stand in his holy place?
⁴ The one who has clean hands and a pure heart,

who has not appealed to what is false,
and who has not sworn deceitfully.
⁵ He will receive blessing from the LORD,
and righteousness from the God of his salvation.
⁶ Such is the generation of those who inquire of him,
who seek the face of the God of Jacob.   *Selah*

JOHN 3:1-21

JESUS AND NICODEMUS

¹ There was a man from the Pharisees named Nicodemus, a ruler of the Jews. ² This man came to him at night and said, "Rabbi, we know that you are a teacher who has come from God, for no one could perform these signs you do unless God were with him."

³ Jesus replied, "Truly I tell you, unless someone is born again, he cannot see the kingdom of God."

⁴ "How can anyone be born when he is old?" Nicodemus asked him. "Can he enter his mother's womb a second time and be born?"

⁵ Jesus answered, "Truly I tell you, unless someone is born of water and the Spirit, he cannot enter the kingdom of God. ⁶ Whatever is born of the flesh is flesh, and whatever is born of the Spirit is spirit. ⁷ Do not be amazed that I told you that you must be born again. ⁸ The wind blows where it pleases, and you hear its sound, but you don't know where it comes from or where it is going. So it is with everyone born of the Spirit."

⁹ "How can these things be?" asked Nicodemus.

¹⁰ "Are you a teacher of Israel and don't know these things?" Jesus replied. ¹¹ "Truly I tell you, we speak what we know and we testify to what we have seen, but you do not accept our testimony. ¹² If I have told you about earthly things and you don't believe, how will you believe if I tell you about heavenly things? ¹³ No one has ascended into heaven except the one who descended from heaven—the Son of Man.

¹⁴ "Just as Moses lifted up the snake in the wilderness, so the Son of Man must be lifted up, ¹⁵ so that everyone who believes in him may have eternal life. ¹⁶ For God loved the world in this way: He gave his one and only Son, so that everyone who believes in him will not perish but have eternal life. ¹⁷ For God did not send his Son into the world to condemn the world, but to save the world through him. ¹⁸ Anyone who believes in him is not condemned, but anyone who does not believe is already condemned, because he has not believed in the name of the one and only Son of God. ¹⁹ This is the judgment: The light has come into the world, and people loved darkness rather than the light because their deeds were evil. ²⁰ For everyone who does evil hates the light and avoids it, so that his deeds may not be exposed. ²¹ But anyone who lives by the truth comes to the light, so that his works may be shown to be accomplished by God."

By Faith

NOAH BUILT

By faith Noah, after he was warned about what
was not yet seen and motivated by godly fear,
built an ark to deliver his family. By faith he
condemned the world and became an heir of the
righteousness that comes by faith.

HEBREWS 11:7

DAY   09

GENESIS 6:5-22

JUDGMENT DECREED

5 When the LORD saw that human wickedness was widespread on the earth and that every inclination of the human mind was nothing but evil all the time, 6 the LORD regretted that he had made man on the earth, and he was deeply grieved. 7 Then the LORD said, "I will wipe mankind, whom I created, off the face of the earth, together with the animals, creatures that crawl, and birds of the sky—for I regret that I made them." 8 Noah, however, found favor with the LORD.

GOD WARNS NOAH

9 These are the family records of Noah. Noah was a righteous man, blameless among his contemporaries; Noah walked with God. 10 And Noah fathered three sons: Shem, Ham, and Japheth.

11 Now the earth was corrupt in God's sight, and the earth was filled with wickedness. 12 God saw how corrupt the earth was, for every creature had corrupted its way on the earth. 13 Then God said to Noah, "I have decided to put an end to every creature, for the earth is filled with wickedness because of them; therefore I am going to destroy them along with the earth.

14 "Make yourself an ark of gopher wood. Make rooms in the ark, and cover it with pitch inside and outside. 15 This is how you are to make it: The ark will be 450 feet long, 75 feet wide, and 45 feet high. 16 You are to make a roof, finishing the sides of the ark to within eighteen inches of the roof. You are to put a door in the side of the ark. Make it with lower, middle, and upper decks.

¹⁷ "Understand that I am bringing a flood—floodwaters on the earth to destroy every creature under heaven with the breath of life in it. Everything on earth will perish. ¹⁸ But I will establish my covenant with you, and you will enter the ark with your sons, your wife, and your sons' wives. ¹⁹ You are also to bring into the ark two of all the living creatures, male and female, to keep them alive with you. ²⁰ Two of everything—from the birds according to their kinds, from the livestock according to their kinds, and from the animals that crawl on the ground according to their kinds—will come to you so that you can keep them alive. ²¹ Take with you every kind of food that is eaten; gather it as food for you and for them." ²² And Noah did this. He did everything that God had commanded him.

GENESIS 7:1-5

ENTERING THE ARK

¹ Then the LORD said to Noah, "Enter the ark, you and all your household, for I have seen that you alone are righteous before me in this generation. ² You are to take with you seven pairs, a male and its female, of all the clean animals, and two of the animals that are not clean, a male and its female, ³ and seven pairs, male and female, of the birds of the sky—in order to keep offspring alive throughout the earth. ⁴ Seven days from now I will make it rain on the earth forty days and forty nights, and every living thing I have made I will wipe off the face of the earth." ⁵ And Noah did everything that the LORD commanded him.

GENESIS 8:15-22

THE LORD'S PROMISE

¹⁵ Then God spoke to Noah, ¹⁶ "Come out of the ark, you, your wife, your sons, and your sons' wives with you. ¹⁷ Bring out all the living creatures that are with you—birds, livestock, those that crawl on the earth—and they will spread over the earth and be fruitful and multiply on the earth." ¹⁸ So Noah, along with his sons, his wife, and his sons' wives, came out. ¹⁹ All the animals, all the creatures that crawl, and all the flying creatures—everything that moves on the earth—came out of the ark by their families.

²⁰ Then Noah built an altar to the LORD. He took some of every kind of clean animal and every kind of clean bird and offered burnt offerings on the

altar. [21] When the Lord smelled the pleasing aroma, he said to himself, "I will never again curse the ground because of human beings, even though the inclination of the human heart is evil from youth onward. And I will never again strike down every living thing as I have done.

> [22] As long as the earth endures,
> seedtime and harvest, cold and heat,
> summer and winter, and day and night
> will not cease."

GENESIS 9:1-17

GOD'S COVENANT WITH NOAH

[1] God blessed Noah and his sons and said to them, "Be fruitful and multiply and fill the earth. [2] The fear and terror of you will be in every living creature on the earth, every bird of the sky, every creature that crawls on the ground, and all the fish of the sea. They are placed under your authority. [3] Every creature that lives and moves will be food for you; as I gave the green plants, I have given you everything. [4] However, you must not eat meat with its lifeblood in it. [5] And I will require a penalty for your lifeblood; I will require it from any animal and from any human; if someone murders a fellow human, I will require that person's life.

> [6] Whoever sheds human blood,
> by humans his blood will be shed,
> for God made humans in his image.

[7] But you, be fruitful and multiply; spread out over the earth and multiply on it."

[8] Then God said to Noah and his sons with him, [9] "Understand that I am establishing my covenant with you and your descendants after you, [10] and with every living creature that is with you—birds, livestock, and all wildlife of the earth that are with you—all the animals of the earth that came out of the ark. [11] I establish my covenant with you that never again will every creature be wiped out by floodwaters; there will never again be a flood to destroy the earth."

¹² And God said, "This is the sign of the covenant I am making between me and you and every living creature with you, a covenant for all future generations: ¹³ I have placed my bow in the clouds, and it will be a sign of the covenant between me and the earth. ¹⁴ Whenever I form clouds over the earth and the bow appears in the clouds, ¹⁵ I will remember my covenant between me and you and all the living creatures: water will never again become a flood to destroy every creature. ¹⁶ The bow will be in the clouds, and I will look at it and remember the permanent covenant between God and all the living creatures on earth." ¹⁷ God said to Noah, "This is the sign of the covenant that I have established between me and every creature on earth."

♥ GOING DEEPER

PSALM 33:13-22

¹³ The LORD looks down from heaven;
he observes everyone.
¹⁴ He gazes on all the inhabitants of the earth
from his dwelling place.
¹⁵ He forms the hearts of them all;
he considers all their works.
¹⁶ A king is not saved by a large army;
a warrior will not be rescued by great strength.
¹⁷ The horse is a false hope for safety;
it provides no escape by its great power.

¹⁸ But look, the LORD keeps his eye on those who fear him—
those who depend on his faithful love
¹⁹ to rescue them from death
and to keep them alive in famine.

²⁰ We wait for the LORD;
he is our help and shield.
²¹ For our hearts rejoice in him
because we trust in his holy name.
²² May your faithful love rest on us, LORD,
for we put our hope in you.

LIVE BY FAITH: A STUDY OF HEBREWS 11

By Faith

ABRAHAM OBEYED

By faith Abraham, when he was called, obeyed and set out for a place that he was going to receive as an inheritance. He went out, even though he did not know where he was going.

HEBREWS 11:8

GENESIS 11:27-32

27 These are the family records of Terah. Terah fathered Abram, Nahor, and Haran, and Haran fathered Lot. 28 Haran died in his native land, in Ur of the Chaldeans, during his father Terah's lifetime. 29 Abram and Nahor took wives: Abram's wife was named Sarai, and Nahor's wife was named Milcah. She was the daughter of Haran, the father of both Milcah and Iscah. 30 Sarai was unable to conceive; she did not have a child.

31 Terah took his son Abram, his grandson Lot (Haran's son), and his daughter-in-law Sarai, his son Abram's wife, and they set out together from Ur of the Chaldeans to go to the land of Canaan. But when they came to Haran, they settled there. 32 Terah lived 205 years and died in Haran.

GENESIS 12:1-9

THE CALL OF ABRAM

¹ The LORD said to Abram:

> Go from your land,
> your relatives,
> and your father's house
> to the land that I will show you.
> ² I will make you into a great nation,
> I will bless you,
> I will make your name great,
> and you will be a blessing.
> ³ I will bless those who bless you,
> I will curse anyone who treats you with contempt,
> and all the peoples on earth
> will be blessed through you.

⁴ So Abram went, as the LORD had told him, and Lot went with him. Abram was seventy-five years old when he left Haran. ⁵ He took his wife, Sarai, his nephew Lot, all the possessions they had accumulated, and the people they had acquired in Haran, and they set out for the land of Canaan. When they came to the land of Canaan, ⁶ Abram passed through the land to the site of Shechem, at the oak of Moreh. (At that time the Canaanites were in the land.) ⁷ The LORD appeared to Abram and said, "To your offspring I will give this land." So he built an altar there to the LORD who had appeared to him. ⁸ From there he moved on to the hill country east of Bethel and pitched his tent, with Bethel on the west and Ai on the east. He built an altar to the LORD there, and he called on the name of the LORD. ⁹ Then Abram journeyed by stages to the Negev.

GENESIS 15:1-6

THE ABRAHAMIC COVENANT

¹ After these events, the word of the LORD came to Abram in a vision:

> Do not be afraid, Abram.
> I am your shield;

your reward will be very great.

² But Abram said, "Lord God, what can you give me, since I am childless and the heir of my house is Eliezer of Damascus?" ³ Abram continued, "Look, you have given me no offspring, so a slave born in my house will be my heir."

⁴ Now the word of the Lord came to him: "This one will not be your heir; instead, one who comes from your own body will be your heir." ⁵ He took him outside and said, "Look at the sky and count the stars, if you are able to count them." Then he said to him, "Your offspring will be that numerous."

⁶ Abram believed the Lord, and he credited it to him as righteousness.

📖 GOING DEEPER

ISAIAH 51:1–2
SALVATION FOR ZION

¹ Listen to me, you who pursue righteousness,
you who seek the Lord:
Look to the rock from which you were cut,
and to the quarry from which you were dug.
² Look to Abraham your father,
and to Sarah who gave birth to you.
When I called him, he was only one;
I blessed him and made him many.

ROMANS 4:1–3
ABRAHAM JUSTIFIED BY FAITH

¹ What then will we say that Abraham, our forefather according to the flesh, has found? ² If Abraham was justified by works, he has something to boast about—but not before God. ³ For what does the Scripture say? Abraham believed God, and it was credited to him for righteousness.

By Faith

ABRAHAM
STAYED

DAY 11

————

By faith he stayed as a foreigner in
the land of promise, living in tents
as did Isaac and Jacob, coheirs of the
same promise. For he was looking forward
to the city that has foundations, whose
architect and builder is God.

HEBREWS 11:9–10

GENESIS 13

ABRAM AND LOT SEPARATE

¹ Abram went up from Egypt to the Negev—he, his wife, and all he had,
and Lot with him. ² Abram was very rich in livestock, silver, and gold.
³ He went by stages from the Negev to Bethel, to the place between
Bethel and Ai where his tent had formerly been, ⁴ to the site where he
had built the altar. And Abram called on the name of the LORD there.

⁵ Now Lot, who was traveling with Abram, also had flocks, herds,
and tents. ⁶ But the land was unable to support them as long as they
stayed together, for they had so many possessions that they could not
stay together, ⁷ and there was quarreling between the herdsmen of
Abram's livestock and the herdsmen of Lot's livestock. (At that time the
Canaanites and the Perizzites were living in the land.)

⁸ So Abram said to Lot, "Please, let's not have quarreling between you
and me, or between your herdsmen and my herdsmen, since we are
relatives. ⁹ Isn't the whole land before you? Separate from me: if you go to
the left, I will go to the right; if you go to the right, I will go to the left."

¹⁰ Lot looked out and saw that the entire plain of the Jordan as far as
Zoar was well watered everywhere like the LORD's garden and the land
of Egypt. (This was before the LORD destroyed Sodom and Gomorrah.)
¹¹ So Lot chose the entire plain of the Jordan for himself. Then Lot
journeyed eastward, and they separated from each other. ¹² Abram lived
in the land of Canaan, but Lot lived in the cities on the plain and set
up his tent near Sodom. ¹³ (Now the men of Sodom were evil, sinning
immensely against the LORD.)

¹⁴ After Lot had separated from him, the LORD said to Abram, "Look
from the place where you are. Look north and south, east and west,

¹⁵ for I will give you and your offspring forever all the land that you see. ¹⁶ I will make your offspring like the dust of the earth, so that if anyone could count the dust of the earth, then your offspring could be counted. ¹⁷ Get up and walk around the land, through its length and width, for I will give it to you."

¹⁸ So Abram moved his tent and went to live near the oaks of Mamre at Hebron, where he built an altar to the LORD.

GENESIS 21:34

And Abraham lived as an alien in the land of the Philistines for many days.

❦ GOING DEEPER

ACTS 7:2-5

² "Brothers and fathers," he replied, "listen: The God of glory appeared to our father Abraham when he was in Mesopotamia, before he settled in Haran, ³ and said to him: Leave your country and relatives, and come to the land that I will show you.

⁴ "Then he left the land of the Chaldeans and settled in Haran. From there, after his father died, God had him move to this land in which you are now living. ⁵ He didn't give him an inheritance in it—not even a foot of ground—but he promised to give it to him as a possession, and to his descendants after him, even though he was childless."

PSALM 27:13-14

¹³ *I am certain that I will see the LORD's goodness in the land of the living.*

¹⁴ Wait for the LORD;
be strong, and let your heart be courageous.
Wait for the LORD.

THE SOLID ROCK

Words: Edward Mote
Music: William B. Bradbury

When darkness seems to hide His face,
I rest on his unchanging grace;
In ev'ry high and stormy gale,
My anchor holds within the veil.

1. My hope is built on noth-ing less than Je-sus's blood and right-eous-ness;
2. When dark-ness seems to hide His face, I rest on His un-chang-ing grace;
3. His oath, His cov-e-nant, His blood sup-port me in the whelm-ing flood;
4. When He shall come with trum-pet sound, Oh, may I then in Him be found;

I dare not trust the sweet-est frame, But whol-ly lean on Je-sus' name.
In ev-'ry high and storm-y gale, My an-chor holds with-in the veil.
When all a-round my soul gives way, He then is all my hope and stay.
Dressed in His right-eous-ness a-lone, Fault-less to stand be-fore the throne.

Chorus

On Christ, the sol-id Rock, I stand; All oth-er ground is

sink-ing sand, All oth-er ground is sink-ing sand.

By Faith

SARAH RECEIVED POWER

By faith even Sarah herself, when she
was unable to have children, received
power to conceive offspring, even
though she was past the age, since
she considered that the one
who had promised was faithful.
Therefore, from one man—in fact, from
one as good as dead—came offspring as
numerous as the stars of the sky and
as innumerable as the grains of sand
along the seashore.

HEBREWS 11:11–12

GENESIS 17:15-22

¹⁵ God said to Abraham, "As for your wife Sarai, do not call her Sarai, for Sarah will be her name. ¹⁶ I will bless her; indeed, I will give you a son by her. I will bless her, and she will produce nations; kings of peoples will come from her."

¹⁷ Abraham fell facedown. Then he laughed and said to himself, "Can a child be born to a hundred-year-old man? Can Sarah, a ninety-year-old woman, give birth?" ¹⁸ So Abraham said to God, "If only Ishmael were acceptable to you!"

¹⁹ But God said, "No. Your wife Sarah will bear you a son, and you will name him Isaac. I will confirm my covenant with him as a permanent covenant for his future offspring. ²⁰ As for Ishmael, I have heard you. I will certainly bless him; I will make him fruitful and will multiply him greatly. He will father twelve tribal leaders, and I will make him into a great nation. ²¹ But I will confirm my covenant with Isaac, whom Sarah will bear to you at this time next year." ²² When he finished talking with him, God withdrew from Abraham.

GENESIS 18:1-15

ABRAHAM'S THREE VISITORS

¹ The LORD appeared to Abraham at the oaks of Mamre while he was sitting at the entrance of his tent during the heat of the day. ² He looked up, and he saw three men standing near him. When he saw them, he ran from the entrance of the tent to meet them, bowed to the ground, ³ and said, "My lord, if I have found favor with you, please do not go on past your servant. ⁴ Let a little water be brought, that you may wash your feet and rest yourselves under the tree. ⁵ I will bring a bit of bread so that you may strengthen yourselves. This is why you have passed your servant's way. Later, you can continue on."

"Yes," they replied, "do as you have said."

⁶ So Abraham hurried into the tent and said to Sarah, "Quick! Knead three measures of fine flour and make bread." ⁷ Abraham ran to the herd and got a tender, choice calf. He gave it to a young man, who hurried to prepare it. ⁸ Then Abraham took curds and milk, as well as the calf that he had prepared, and set them before the men. He served them as they ate under the tree.

⁹ "Where is your wife Sarah?" they asked him.

"There, in the tent," he answered.

¹⁰ The LORD said, "I will certainly come back to you in about a year's time, and your wife Sarah will have a son!" Now Sarah was listening at the entrance of the tent behind him.

¹¹ Abraham and Sarah were old and getting on in years. Sarah had passed the age of childbearing. ¹² So she laughed to herself: "After I am worn out and my lord is old, will I have delight?"

¹³ But the LORD asked Abraham, "Why did Sarah laugh, saying, 'Can I really have a baby when I'm old?' ¹⁴ Is anything impossible for the LORD? At the appointed time I will come back to you, and in about a year she will have a son."

¹⁵ Sarah denied it. "I did not laugh," she said, because she was afraid.

But he replied, "No, you did laugh."

GENESIS 21:1-7

THE BIRTH OF ISAAC

¹ The LORD came to Sarah as he had said, and

the LORD did for Sarah what he had promised.

² Sarah became pregnant and bore a son to Abraham in his old age, at the appointed time God had told him. ³ Abraham named his son who was born to him—the one Sarah bore to him—Isaac. ⁴ When his son Isaac was eight days old, Abraham circumcised him, as God had commanded him. ⁵ Abraham was a hundred years old when his son Isaac was born to him.

⁶ Sarah said, "God has made me laugh, and everyone who hears will laugh with me." ⁷ She also said, "Who would have told Abraham that Sarah would nurse children? Yet I have borne a son for him in his old age."

GOING DEEPER

ROMANS 4:13–25

THE PROMISE GRANTED THROUGH FAITH

[13] For the promise to Abraham or to his descendants that he would inherit the world was not through the law, but through the righteousness that comes by faith. [14] If those who are of the law are heirs, faith is made empty and the promise nullified, [15] because the law produces wrath. And where there is no law, there is no transgression.

[16] This is why the promise is by faith, so that it may be according to grace, to guarantee it to all the descendants—not only to the one who is of the law but also to the one who is of Abraham's faith. He is the father of us all. [17] As it is written: I have made you the father of many nations—in the presence of the God in whom he believed,the one who gives life to the dead and calls things into existence that do not exist. [18] He believed, hoping against hope, so that he became the father of many nations according to what had been spoken: So will your descendants be. [19] He did not weaken in faith when he considered his own body to be already dead (since he was about a hundred years old) and also the deadness of Sarah's womb. [20] He did not waver in unbelief at God's promise but was strengthened in his faith and gave glory to God, [21] because he was fully convinced that what God had promised, he was also able to do. [22] Therefore, it was credited to him for righteousness. [23] Now it was credited to him was not written for Abraham alone, [24] but also for us. It will be credited to us who believe in him who raised Jesus our Lord from the dead. [25] He was delivered up for our trespasses and raised for our justification.

HEBREWS 10:23

Let us hold on to the confession of our hope without wavering, since he who promised is faithful.

02

WEEKLY RESPONSE

Review any notes you took throughout your reading this week. Use them as you answer the following questions, reflecting on how these stories encourage you to respond to God in faith in your own life.

What aspects of God's character stood out to you, challenged you, or encouraged you?

How did the people in this week's stories respond to God?

What surprised you
about their stories?

What parts of their
experiences made it
difficult for them
to respond to God
in faith?

How have you seen God
working in your own
life this week? What
might it look like for
you to respond to Him
in faith?

GRACE DAY

Take this day to catch up on your reading, pray, and rest in the presence of the Lord.

For our hearts rejoice in him because we trust in his holy name. May your faithful love rest on us, LORD, for we put our hope in you.

PSALM 33:21–22

WEEKLY

Scripture is God-breathed and true. When we memorize it, we carry the good news of Jesus with us wherever we go.

For this plan, we are memorizing Hebrews 5:7–9, a passage from this study that summarizes how Jesus is both the firm foundation of our faith and how we are to imitate Jesus's faith in our own response to God. We'll continue by memorizing the second half of verse 7.

SEE TIPS FOR MEMORIZING SCRIPTURE ON PAGE 164.

TRUTH

HEBREWS 5:7-9

7 During his earthly life, he offered prayers and appeals with loud cries and tears to the one who was able to save him from death, and he was heard because of his reverence. 8 Although he was the Son, he learned obedience from what he suffered. 9 After he was perfected, he became the source of eternal salvation for all who obey him…

These All

DIED IN FAITH

These all died in faith, although they had not received the things that were promised. But they saw them from a distance, greeted them, and confessed that they were foreigners and temporary residents on the earth. Now those who say such things make it clear that they are seeking a homeland. If they were thinking about where they came from, they would have had an opportunity to return. But they now desire a better place—a heavenly one. Therefore, God is not ashamed to be called their God, for he has prepared a city for them.

HEBREWS 11:13–16

🔖 GOING DEEPER

ROMANS 8:18-25

FROM GROANS TO GLORY

[18] For I consider that the sufferings of this present time are not worth comparing with the glory that is going to be revealed to us. [19] For the creation eagerly waits with anticipation for God's sons to be revealed.

[20] For the creation was subjected to futility—not willingly, but because of him who subjected it—in the hope [21] that the creation itself will also be set free from the bondage to decay into the glorious freedom of God's children. [22] For we know that the whole creation has been groaning together with labor pains until now. [23] Not only that, but we ourselves who have the Spirit as the firstfruits—we also groan within ourselves, eagerly waiting for adoption, the redemption of our bodies. [24] Now in this hope we were saved, but hope that is seen is not hope, because who hopes for what he sees? [25] Now if we hope for what we do not see, we eagerly wait for it with patience.

2 CORINTHIANS 5:1-9

OUR FUTURE AFTER DEATH

[1] For we know that if our earthly tent we live in is destroyed, we have a building from God, an eternal dwelling in the heavens, not made with hands.

[2] Indeed, we groan in this tent, desiring to put on our heavenly dwelling, [3] since, when we are clothed, we will not be found naked. [4] Indeed, we groan while we are in this tent, burdened as we are, because we do not want to be unclothed but clothed, so that mortality may be swallowed up by life. [5] Now the one who prepared us for this very purpose is God, who gave us the Spirit as a down payment.

[6] So we are always confident and know that while we are at home in the body we are away from the Lord. [7] For we walk by faith, not by sight. [8] In fact, we are confident, and we would prefer to be away from the body and at home with the Lord. [9] Therefore, whether we are at home or away, we make it our aim to be pleasing to him.

ISAIAH 65:17-25

A NEW CREATION

[17] "For I will create new heavens and a new earth;
the past events will not be remembered or come to mind.
[18] Then be glad and rejoice forever
in what I am creating;

for I will create Jerusalem to be a joy
and its people to be a delight.
¹⁹ I will rejoice in Jerusalem
and be glad in my people.
The sound of weeping and crying
will no longer be heard in her.
²⁰ In her, a nursing infant will no longer live
only a few days,
or an old man not live out his days.
Indeed, the one who dies at a hundred years old
will be mourned as a young man,
and the one who misses a hundred years
will be considered cursed.
²¹ People will build houses and live in them;
they will plant vineyards and eat their fruit.
²² They will not build and others live in them;
they will not plant and others eat.
For my people's lives will be
like the lifetime of a tree.
My chosen ones will fully enjoy
the work of their hands.
²³ They will not labor without success
or bear children destined for disaster,
for they will be a people blessed by the LORD
along with their descendants.
²⁴ Even before they call, I will answer;
while they are still speaking, I will hear.
²⁵ The wolf and the lamb will feed together,
and the lion will eat straw like cattle,
but the serpent's food will be dust!
They will not do what is evil or destroy
on my entire holy mountain,"
says the LORD.

By Faith

ABRAHAM
OFFERED

DAY 16

By faith Abraham, when he was tested, offered up Isaac. He received the promises and yet he was offering his one and only son, the one to whom it had been said, Your offspring will be traced through Isaac. He considered God to be able even to raise someone from the dead; therefore, he received him back, figuratively speaking.

HEBREWS 11:17–19

GENESIS 17:1-8

COVENANT CIRCUMCISION

¹ When Abram was ninety-nine years old, the LORD appeared to him, saying, "I am God Almighty. Live in my presence and be blameless. ² I will set up my covenant between me and you, and I will multiply you greatly."

³ Then Abram fell facedown and God spoke with him: ⁴ "As for me, here is my covenant with you: You will become the father of many nations. ⁵ Your name will no longer be Abram; your name will be Abraham, for I will make you the father of many nations. ⁶ I will make you extremely fruitful and will make nations and kings come from you. ⁷ I will confirm my covenant that is between me and you and your future offspring throughout their generations. It is a permanent covenant to be your God and the God of your offspring after you. ⁸ And to you and your future offspring I will give the land where you are residing—all the land of Canaan—as a permanent possession, and I will be their God."

GENESIS 22:1-19

THE SACRIFICE OF ISAAC

¹ After these things God tested Abraham and said to him, "Abraham!"

"Here I am," he answered.

² "Take your son," he said, "your only son Isaac, whom you love, go to the land of Moriah, and offer him there as a burnt offering on one of the mountains I will tell you about."

³ So Abraham got up early in the morning, saddled his donkey, and took with him two of his young men and his son Isaac. He split wood for a burnt offering and set out to go to the place God had told him about. ⁴ On the third day Abraham looked up and saw the place in the distance. ⁵ Then Abraham said to his young men, "Stay here with the donkey. The boy and I will go over there to worship; then we'll come back to you." ⁶ Abraham took the wood for the burnt offering and laid it on his son Isaac. In his hand he took the fire and the knife, and the two of them walked on together.

⁷ Then Isaac spoke to his father Abraham and said, "My father."

And he replied, "Here I am, my son."

Isaac said, "The fire and the wood are here, but where is the lamb for the burnt offering?"

⁸ Abraham answered, "God himself will provide the lamb for the burnt offering, my son." Then the two of them walked on together.

⁹ When they arrived at the place that God had told him about, Abraham built the altar there and arranged the wood. He bound his son Isaac and placed him on the altar on top of the wood. ¹⁰ Then Abraham reached out and took the knife to slaughter his son.

¹¹ But the angel of the LORD called to him from heaven and said, "Abraham, Abraham!"

He replied, "Here I am."

¹² Then he said, "Do not lay a hand on the boy or do anything to him. For now I know that you fear God, since you have not withheld your only son from me." ¹³ Abraham looked up and saw a ram caught in the thicket by its horns. So Abraham went and took the ram and offered it as a burnt offering in place of his son. ¹⁴ And Abraham named that place The LORD Will Provide, so today it is said, "It will be provided on the LORD's mountain."

¹⁵ Then the angel of the Lord called to Abraham a second time from heaven ¹⁶ and said, "By myself I have sworn," this is the Lord's declaration: "Because you have done this thing and have not withheld your only son, ¹⁷ I will indeed bless you and make your offspring as numerous as the stars of the sky and the sand on the seashore. Your offspring will possess the city gates of their enemies.

¹⁸ And all the nations of the earth will be blessed by your offspring because you have obeyed my command."

¹⁹ Abraham went back to his young men, and they got up and went together to Beer-sheba. And Abraham settled in Beer-sheba.

◣ GOING DEEPER

JAMES 2:21-23

²¹ Wasn't Abraham our father justified by works in offering Isaac his son on the altar? ²² You see that faith was active together with his works, and by works, faith was made complete, ²³ and the Scripture was fulfilled that says Abraham believed God, and it was credited to him as righteousness, and he was called God's friend.

1 JOHN 5:1-4

¹ Everyone who believes that Jesus is the Christ has been born of God, and everyone who loves the Father also loves the one born of him. ² This is how we know that we love God's children: when we love God and obey his commands. ³ For this is what love for God is: to keep his commands. And his commands are not a burden, ⁴ because everyone who has been born of God conquers the world. This is the victory that has conquered the world: our faith.

By Faith

ISAAC BLESSED

By faith Isaac blessed Jacob and
Esau concerning things to come.

HEBREWS 11:20

DAY   17

GENESIS 27:1-40

THE STOLEN BLESSING

¹ When Isaac was old and his eyes were so weak that he could not see, he called his older son Esau and said to him, "My son."

And he answered, "Here I am."

² He said, "Look, I am old and do not know the day of my death. ³ So now take your hunting gear, your quiver and bow, and go out in the field to hunt some game for me. ⁴ Then make me a delicious meal that I love and bring it to me to eat, so that I can bless you before I die."

⁵ Now Rebekah was listening to what Isaac said to his son Esau. So while Esau went to the field to hunt some game to bring in, ⁶ Rebekah said to her son Jacob, "Listen! I heard your father talking with your brother Esau. He said, ⁷ 'Bring me game and make a delicious meal for me to eat so that I can bless you in the LORD's presence before I die.' ⁸ Now, my son, listen to me and do what I tell you. ⁹ Go to

the flock and bring me two choice young goats, and I will make them into a delicious meal for your father—the kind he loves. ¹⁰ Then take it to your father to eat so that he may bless you before he dies."

¹¹ Jacob answered Rebekah his mother, "Look, my brother Esau is a hairy man, but I am a man with smooth skin. ¹² Suppose my father touches me. Then I will be revealed to him as a deceiver and bring a curse rather than a blessing on myself."

¹³ His mother said to him, "Your curse be on me, my son. Just obey me and go get them for me."

¹⁴ So he went and got the goats and brought them to his mother, and his mother made the delicious food his father loved. ¹⁵ Then Rebekah took the best clothes of her older son Esau, which were in the house, and had her younger

son Jacob wear them. ¹⁶ She put the skins of the young goats on his hands and the smooth part of his neck. ¹⁷ Then she handed the delicious food and the bread she had made to her son Jacob.

¹⁸ When he came to his father, he said, "My father."

And he answered, "Here I am. Who are you, my son?"

¹⁹ Jacob replied to his father, "I am Esau, your firstborn. I have done as you told me. Please sit up and eat some of my game so that you may bless me."

²⁰ But Isaac said to his son, "How did you ever find it so quickly, my son?"

He replied, "Because the LORD your God made it happen for me."

²¹ Then Isaac said to Jacob, "Please come closer so I can touch you, my son. Are you really my son Esau or not?"

²² So Jacob came closer to his father Isaac. When he touched him, he said, "The voice is the voice of Jacob, but the hands are the hands of Esau." ²³ He did not recognize him, because his hands were hairy like those of his brother Esau; so he blessed him. ²⁴ Again he asked, "Are you really my son Esau?"

And he replied, "I am."

²⁵ Then he said, "Bring it closer to me, and let me eat some of my son's game so that I can bless you." Jacob brought it closer to him, and he ate; he brought him wine, and he drank.

²⁶ Then his father Isaac said to him, "Please come closer and kiss me, my son." ²⁷ So he came closer and kissed him. When Isaac smelled his clothes, he blessed him and said:

Ah, the smell of my son
is like the smell of a field
that the LORD has blessed.
²⁸ May God give to you—
from the dew of the sky

and from the richness of the land—
an abundance of grain and new wine.
[29] May peoples serve you
and nations bow in homage to you.
Be master over your relatives;
may your mother's sons bow in homage to you.
Those who curse you will be cursed,
and those who bless you will be blessed.

[30] As soon as Isaac had finished blessing Jacob and Jacob had left the presence of his father Isaac, his brother Esau arrived from his hunting. [31] He had also made some delicious food and brought it to his father. He said to his father, "Let my father get up and eat some of his son's game, so that you may bless me."

[32] But his father Isaac said to him, "Who are you?"

He answered, "I am Esau your firstborn son."

[33] Isaac began to tremble uncontrollably. "Who was it then," he said, "who hunted game and brought it to me? I ate it all before you came in, and I blessed him. Indeed, he will be blessed!"

[34] When Esau heard his father's words, he cried out with a loud and bitter cry and said to his father, "Bless me too, my father!"

[35] But he replied, "Your brother came deceitfully and took your blessing."

[36] So he said, "Isn't he rightly named Jacob? For he has cheated me twice now. He took my birthright, and look, now he has taken my blessing." Then he asked, "Haven't you saved a blessing for me?"

[37] But Isaac answered Esau, "Look, I have made him a master over you, have given him all of his relatives as his servants, and have sustained him with grain and new wine. What then can I do for you, my son?"

[38] Esau said to his father, "Do you have only one blessing, my father? Bless me too, my father!" And Esau wept loudly.

³⁹ His father Isaac answered him,

Look, your dwelling place will be
away from the richness of the land,
away from the dew of the sky above.
⁴⁰ You will live by your sword,
and you will serve your brother.
But when you rebel,
you will break his yoke from your neck.

GOING DEEPER

PSALM 37:22-29

²² Those who are blessed by the LORD will inherit the land,
but those cursed by him will be destroyed.

²³ A person's steps are established by the LORD,
and he takes pleasure in his way.
²⁴ Though he falls, he will not be overwhelmed,
because the LORD supports him with his hand.

²⁵ I have been young and now I am old,
yet I have not seen the righteous abandoned
or his children begging for bread.
²⁶ He is always generous, always lending,
and his children are a blessing.

²⁷ Turn away from evil, do what is good,
and settle permanently.
²⁸ For the LORD loves justice
and will not abandon his faithful ones.
They are kept safe forever,
but the children of the wicked will be destroyed.
²⁹ The righteous will inherit the land
and dwell in it permanently.

By Faith

JACOB BLESSED
AND WORSHIPED

———

By faith Jacob, when he was dying,
blessed each of the sons of Joseph,
and he worshiped, leaning on the
top of his staff.

HEBREWS 11:21

DAY   18

JACOB BLESSES EPHRAIM AND MANASSEH

[1] Some time after this, Joseph was told, "Your father is weaker." So he set out with his two sons, Manasseh and Ephraim. [2] When Jacob was told, "Your son Joseph has come to you," Israel summoned his strength and sat up in bed.

[3] Jacob said to Joseph, "God Almighty appeared to me at Luz in the land of Canaan and blessed me. [4] He said to me, 'I will make you fruitful and numerous; I will make many nations come from you, and I will give this land as a permanent possession to your future descendants.' [5] Your two sons born to you in the land of Egypt before I came to you in Egypt are now mine. Ephraim and Manasseh belong to me just as Reuben and Simeon do. [6] Children born to you after them will be yours and will be recorded under the names of their brothers with regard to their inheritance. [7] When I was returning from Paddan, to my sorrow Rachel died along the way, some distance from Ephrath in the land of Canaan. I buried her there along the way to Ephrath" (that is, Bethlehem).

[8] When Israel saw Joseph's sons, he said, "Who are these?"

[9] And Joseph said to his father, "They are my sons God has given me here."

So Israel said, "Bring them to me and I will bless them." [10] Now his eyesight was poor because of old age; he could hardly see. Joseph brought them to him, and he kissed and embraced them. [11] Israel said to Joseph, "I never expected to see your face again, but now God has even let me see your offspring." [12] Then Joseph took them from his father's knees and bowed with his face to the ground.

EPHRAIM'S GREATER BLESSING

[13] Then Joseph took them both—with his right hand Ephraim toward Israel's left, and with his left hand Manasseh toward Israel's right—and brought them to Israel. [14] But Israel stretched out his right hand and put it on the head of Ephraim, the younger, and crossing his hands, put his left on Manasseh's head, although Manasseh was the firstborn. [15] Then he blessed Joseph and said:

The God before whom my fathers Abraham and Isaac walked,
the God who has been my shepherd all my life to this day,

16 the angel who has redeemed me from
all harm—
may he bless these boys.
And may they be called by my name
and the names of my fathers Abraham
and Isaac,
and may they grow to be numerous within
the land.

17 When Joseph saw that his father had placed his right hand on Ephraim's head, he thought it was a mistake and took his father's hand to move it from Ephraim's head to Manasseh's. 18 Joseph said to his father, "Not that way, my father! This one is the firstborn. Put your right hand on his head."

19 But his father refused and said, "I know, my son, I know! He too will become a tribe, and he too will be great; nevertheless, his younger brother will be greater than he, and his offspring will become a populous nation." 20 So he blessed them that day, putting Ephraim before Manasseh when he said, "The nation Israel will invoke blessings by you, saying, 'May God make you like Ephraim and Manasseh.'"

21 Israel said to Joseph, "Look, I am about to die, but God will be with you and will bring you back to the land of your fathers. 22 Over and above what I am giving your brothers, I am giving you the one mountain slope that I took from the Amorites with my sword and bow."

⬛ GOING DEEPER

PSALM 77:13–15

13 God, your way is holy.
What god is great like God?
14 You are the God who works wonders;
you revealed your strength among the peoples.
15 With power you redeemed your people,
the descendants of Jacob and Joseph.   *Selah*

ISAIAH 29:22–23

22 Therefore, the LORD who redeemed Abraham says this about the house of Jacob:

Jacob will no longer be ashamed,
and his face will no longer be pale.

*23 For when he sees his children,
the work of my hands within
his nation,
they will honor my name,*

they will honor the Holy One of Jacob
and stand in awe of the God of Israel.

ROMANS 12:1

Therefore, brothers and sisters, in view of the mercies of God, I urge you to present your bodies as a living sacrifice, holy and pleasing to God; this is your true worship.

———

BLESSED ASSURANCE, JESUS IS MINE

Words: Fanny J. Crosby
Music: Phoebe Palmer Knapp

```
       Blessed assurance, Jesus is mine!
      Oh, what a foretaste of glory divine!
       Heir of salvation, purchase of God,
    Born of his Spirit, washed in his blood.
```

1. Bless-ed as-sur-ance, Je-sus is mine! Oh, what a fore-taste of
2. Per-fect sub-mis-sion, per-fect de-light, Vi-sions of rap-ture now
3. Per-fect sub-mis-sion, all is at rest, I in my Sav-ior am

glo-ry di-vine! Heir of sal-va-tion, pur-chase of God,
burst on my sight: An-gels de-scend-ing bring from a-bove
hap-py and blest; Watch-ing and wait-ing, look-ing a-bove,

Chorus

Born of His Spir-it, washed in His blood.
Ech-oes of mer-cy, whis-pers of love. This is my sto-ry, this is my
Filled with His good-ness, lost in His love.

song, Prais-ing my Sav-ior all the day long; This is my sto-ry,

this is my song, Prais-ing my Sav-ior all the day long.

By Faith

JOSEPH GAVE INSTRUCTIONS

By faith Joseph, as he was nearing
the end of his life, mentioned the
exodus of the Israelites and gave
instructions concerning his bones.

HEBREWS 11:22

GENESIS 50:22-26

JOSEPH'S DEATH

²² Joseph and his father's family remained in Egypt. Joseph lived 110 years. ²³ He saw Ephraim's sons to the third generation; the sons of Manasseh's son Machir were recognized by Joseph.

²⁴ Joseph said to his brothers,

"I am about to die, but God will certainly come to your aid and bring you up from this land to the land he swore to give to Abraham, Isaac, and Jacob."

²⁵ So Joseph made the sons of Israel take an oath: "When God comes to your aid, you are to carry my bones up from here."

²⁶ Joseph died at the age of 110. They embalmed him and placed him in a coffin in Egypt.

EXODUS 13:19

Moses took the bones of Joseph with him, because Joseph had made the Israelites swear a solemn oath, saying, "God will certainly come to your aid; then you must take my bones with you from this place."

◗ GOING DEEPER

ISAIAH 25:7-9

⁷ On this mountain
he will swallow up the burial shroud,
the shroud over all the peoples,
the sheet covering all the nations.
⁸ When he has swallowed up death once and for all,
the Lord God will wipe away the tears

from every face
and remove his people's disgrace
from the whole earth,
for the Lord has spoken.

⁹ On that day it will be said,
"Look, this is our God;
we have waited for him, and he has saved us.
This is the Lord; we have waited for him.
Let's rejoice and be glad in his salvation."

2 CORINTHIANS 4:7–18

TREASURE IN CLAY JARS

⁷ Now we have this treasure in clay jars, so that this extraordinary power may be from God and not from us. ⁸ We are afflicted in every way but not crushed; we are perplexed but not in despair; ⁹ we are persecuted but not abandoned; we are struck down but not destroyed. ¹⁰ We always carry the death of Jesus in our body, so that the life of Jesus may also be displayed in our body. ¹¹ For we who live are always being given over to death for Jesus's sake, so that Jesus's life may also be displayed in our mortal flesh. ¹² So then, death is at work in us, but life in you. ¹³ And since we have the same spirit of faith in keeping with what is written, I believed, therefore I spoke, we also believe, and therefore speak. ¹⁴ For we know that the one who raised the Lord Jesus will also raise us with Jesus and present us with you. ¹⁵ Indeed, everything is for your benefit so that, as grace extends through more and more people, it may cause thanksgiving to increase to the glory of God.

¹⁶ Therefore we do not give up. Even though our outer person is being destroyed, our inner person is being renewed day by day. ¹⁷ For our momentary light affliction is producing for us an absolutely incomparable eternal weight of glory. ¹⁸ So we do not focus on what is seen, but on what is unseen. For what is seen is temporary, but what is unseen is eternal.

WEEKLY RESPONSE

03

Review any notes you took throughout your reading this week. Use them as you answer the following questions, reflecting on how these stories encourage you to respond to God in faith in your own life.

What aspects of God's character stood out to you, challenged you, or encouraged you?

How did the people in this week's stories respond to God?

What surprised you
about their stories?

What parts of their
experiences made it
difficult for them
to respond to God
in faith?

How have you seen God
working in your own
life this week? What
might it look like for
you to respond to Him
in faith?

GRACE DAY

Take this day to catch up on your reading, pray, and rest in the presence of the Lord.

_____

For this is what love for God is: to keep his commands. And his commands are not a burden, because everyone who has been born of God conquers the world. This is the victory that has conquered the world: our faith.

1 JOHN 5:3–4

_____

WEEKLY

DAY ————————————————

Scripture is God-breathed and true. When we memorize it,
we carry the good news of Jesus with us wherever we go.

For this plan, we are memorizing Hebrews 5:7–9, a passage
from this study that summarizes how Jesus is both the firm
foundation of our faith and how we are to imitate Jesus's faith in
our own response to God. This week, we'll memorize verse 8.

SEE TIPS FOR MEMORIZING SCRIPTURE ON PAGE 164.

TRUTH

7 During his earthly life, he offered prayers and appeals with loud cries and tears to the one who was able to save him from death, and he was heard because of his reverence. 8 Although he was the Son, he learned obedience from what he suffered. 9 After he was perfected, he became the source of eternal salvation for all who obey him…

By Faith

MOSES WAS HIDDEN

DAY 22

By faith Moses, after he was born, was
hidden by his parents for three months,
because they saw that the child was
beautiful, and they didn't fear the
king's edict.

HEBREWS 11:23

EXODUS 1

ISRAEL OPPRESSED IN EGYPT

¹ These are the names of the sons of Israel who came to Egypt with Jacob;
each came with his family:

²   Reuben, Simeon, Levi, and Judah;
³   Issachar, Zebulun, and Benjamin;
⁴   Dan and Naphtali; Gad and Asher.

⁵ The total number of Jacob's descendants was seventy; Joseph was already
in Egypt.

⁶ Joseph and all his brothers and all that generation eventually died.
⁷ But the Israelites were fruitful, increased rapidly, multiplied, and
became extremely numerous so that the land was filled with them.

⁸ A new king, who did not know about Joseph, came to power in Egypt.
⁹ He said to his people, "Look, the Israelite people are more numerous and
powerful than we are. ¹⁰ Come, let's deal shrewdly with them; otherwise
they will multiply further, and when war breaks out, they will join our
enemies, fight against us, and leave the country." ¹¹ So the Egyptians
assigned taskmasters over the Israelites to oppress them with forced labor.
They built Pithom and Rameses as supply cities for Pharaoh. ¹² But the
more they oppressed them, the more they multiplied and spread so that
the Egyptians came to dread the Israelites. ¹³ They worked the Israelites
ruthlessly ¹⁴ and made their lives bitter with difficult labor in brick and
mortar and in all kinds of fieldwork. They ruthlessly imposed all this
work on them.

¹⁵ The king of Egypt said to the Hebrew midwives—the first, whose name
was Shiphrah, and the second, whose name was Puah— ¹⁶ "When you

help the Hebrew women give birth, observe them as they deliver. If the child is a son, kill him, but if it's a daughter, she may live." [17] The midwives, however, feared God and did not do as the king of Egypt had told them; they let the boys live. [18] So the king of Egypt summoned the midwives and asked them, "Why have you done this and let the boys live?"

[19] The midwives said to Pharaoh, "The Hebrew women are not like the Egyptian women, for they are vigorous and give birth before the midwife can get to them."

[20] So God was good to the midwives, and the people multiplied and became very numerous. [21] Since the midwives feared God, he gave them families. [22] Pharaoh then commanded all his people, "You must throw every son born to the Hebrews into the Nile, but let every daughter live."

EXODUS 2:1-4

[1] Now a man from the family of Levi married a Levite woman. [2] The woman became pregnant and gave birth to a son; when she saw that he was beautiful, she hid him for three months. [3] But when she could no longer hide him, she got a papyrus basket for him and coated it with asphalt and pitch. She placed the child in it and set it among the reeds by the bank of the Nile. [4] Then his sister stood at a distance in order to see what would happen to him.

♥ GOING DEEPER

PSALM 31:19-24

[19] How great is your goodness,
which you have stored up for those who fear you.
In the presence of everyone you have acted
for those who take refuge in you.
[20] You hide them in the protection of your presence;
you conceal them in a shelter
from human schemes,
from quarrelsome tongues.
[21] Blessed be the LORD,

for he has wondrously shown his faithful love to me
in a city under siege.
²² In my alarm I said,
"I am cut off from your sight."
But you heard the sound of my pleading
when I cried to you for help.

²³ Love the LORD, all his faithful ones.
The LORD protects the loyal,
but fully repays the arrogant.
²⁴ Be strong, and let your heart be courageous,
all you who put your hope in the LORD.

PSALM 118:6-9

⁶ The LORD is for me; I will not be afraid.
What can a mere mortal do to me?
⁷ The LORD is my helper;
therefore, I will look in triumph on those who hate me.

⁸ It is better to take refuge in the LORD
than to trust in humanity.
⁹ It is better to take refuge in the LORD
than to trust in nobles.

LUKE 12:4-7

FEAR GOD

⁴ "I say to you, my friends, don't fear those who kill the body, and after that can do nothing more. ⁵ But I will show you the one to fear: Fear him who has authority to throw people into hell after death. Yes, I say to you, this is the one to fear! ⁶ Aren't five sparrows sold for two pennies? Yet not one of them is forgotten in God's sight. ⁷ Indeed, the hairs of your head are all counted.

Don't be afraid; you are worth more than many sparrows."

By Faith

MOSES CHOSE
TO SUFFER

By faith Moses, when he had grown up, refused to be
called the son of Pharaoh's daughter and chose to
suffer with the people of God rather than to enjoy
the fleeting pleasure of sin. For he considered
reproach for the sake of Christ to be greater
wealth than the treasures of Egypt, since he was
looking ahead to the reward.

By faith he left Egypt behind, not being afraid of
the king's anger, for Moses persevered as one who
sees him who is invisible.

HEBREWS 11:24–27

DAY   2 3

EXODUS 2:5-15

5 Pharaoh's daughter went down to bathe at the Nile while her servant girls walked along the riverbank. She saw the basket among the reeds, sent her slave girl, took it, 6 opened it, and saw him, the child—and there he was, a little boy, crying. She felt sorry for him and said, "This is one of the Hebrew boys."

7 Then his sister said to Pharaoh's daughter, "Should I go and call a Hebrew woman who is nursing to nurse the boy for you?"

8 "Go," Pharaoh's daughter told her. So the girl went and called the boy's mother. 9 Then Pharaoh's daughter said to her, "Take this child and nurse him for me, and I will pay your wages." So the woman took the boy and nursed him. 10 When the child grew older, she brought him to Pharaoh's daughter, and he became her son. She named him Moses, "Because," she said, "I drew him out of the water."

MOSES IN MIDIAN

11 Years later, after Moses had grown up, he went out to his own people and observed their forced labor. He saw an Egyptian striking a Hebrew, one of his people. 12 Looking all around and seeing no one, he struck the

Egyptian dead and hid him in the sand. [13] The next day he went out and saw two Hebrews fighting. He asked the one in the wrong, "Why are you attacking your neighbor?"

[14] "Who made you a commander and judge over us?" the man replied. "Are you planning to kill me as you killed the Egyptian?"

Then Moses became afraid and thought, "What I did is certainly known."

[15] When Pharaoh heard about this, he tried to kill Moses. But Moses fled from Pharaoh and went to live in the land of Midian, and sat down by a well.

EXODUS 4:19-20

[19] Now in Midian the LORD told Moses, "Return to Egypt, for all the men who wanted to kill you are dead." [20] So Moses took his wife and sons, put them on a donkey, and returned to the land of Egypt. And Moses took God's staff in his hand.

EXODUS 5

MOSES CONFRONTS PHARAOH

[1] Later, Moses and Aaron went in and said to Pharaoh, "This is what the LORD, the God of Israel, says: Let my people go, so that they may hold a festival for me in the wilderness."

[2] But Pharaoh responded, "Who is the LORD that I should obey him by letting Israel go? I don't know the LORD, and besides, I will not let Israel go."

[3] They answered, "The God of the Hebrews has met with us. Please let us go on a three-day trip into the wilderness so that we may sacrifice to the LORD our God, or else he may strike us with plague or sword."

[4] The king of Egypt said to them, "Moses and Aaron, why are you causing the people to neglect their work? Get to your labor!" [5] Pharaoh also said, "Look, the people of the land are so numerous, and you would stop them from their labor."

FURTHER OPPRESSION OF ISRAEL

⁶ That day Pharaoh commanded the overseers of the people as well as their foremen, ⁷ "Don't continue to supply the people with straw for making bricks, as before. They must go and gather straw for themselves. ⁸ But require the same quota of bricks from them as they were making before; do not reduce it. For they are slackers—that is why they are crying out, 'Let us go and sacrifice to our God.' ⁹ Impose heavier work on the men. Then they will be occupied with it and not pay attention to deceptive words."

¹⁰ So the overseers and foremen of the people went out and said to them, "This is what Pharaoh says: 'I am not giving you straw. ¹¹ Go get straw yourselves wherever you can find it, but there will be no reduction at all in your workload.'" ¹² So the people scattered throughout the land of Egypt to gather stubble for straw. ¹³ The overseers insisted, "Finish your assigned work each day, just as you did when straw was provided." ¹⁴ Then the Israelite foremen, whom Pharaoh's slave drivers had set over the people, were beaten and asked, "Why haven't you finished making your prescribed number of bricks yesterday or today, as you did before?"

¹⁵ So the Israelite foremen went in and cried for help to Pharaoh: "Why are you treating your servants this way? ¹⁶ No straw has been given to your servants, yet they say to us, 'Make bricks!' Look, your servants are being beaten, but it is your own people who are at fault."

¹⁷ But he said, "You are slackers. Slackers! That is why you are saying, 'Let us go sacrifice to the LORD.' ¹⁸ Now get to work. No straw will be given to you, but you must produce the same quantity of bricks."

¹⁹ The Israelite foremen saw that they were in trouble when they were told, "You cannot reduce your daily quota of bricks." ²⁰ When they left Pharaoh, they confronted Moses and Aaron, who stood waiting to meet them.

²¹ "May the LORD take note of you and judge," they said to them, "because you have made us reek to Pharaoh and his officials—putting a sword in their hand to kill us!"

²² So Moses went back to the LORD and asked, "Lord, why have you caused trouble for this people? And why did you ever send me? ²³ Ever since I went in to Pharaoh to speak in your name he has caused trouble for this people, and you haven't rescued your people at all."

◥ GOING DEEPER

1 PETER 4:12-19

CHRISTIAN SUFFERING

¹² Dear friends, don't be surprised when the fiery ordeal comes among you to test you, as if something unusual were happening to you. ¹³ Instead, rejoice as you share in the sufferings of Christ, so that you may also rejoice with great joy when his glory is revealed. ¹⁴ If you are ridiculed for the name of Christ, you are blessed, because the Spirit of glory and of God rests on you. ¹⁵ Let none of you suffer as a murderer, a thief, an evildoer, or a meddler. ¹⁶ But if anyone suffers as a Christian, let him not be ashamed but let him glorify God in having that name. ¹⁷ For the time has come for judgment to begin with God's household, and if it begins with us, what will the outcome be for those who disobey the gospel of God?

¹⁸ And if a righteous person is saved with difficulty,
what will become of the ungodly and the sinner?

¹⁹ So then, let those who suffer according to God's will entrust themselves to a faithful Creator while doing what is good.

—

IT IS WELL WITH MY SOUL

Words: Horatio G. Spafford
Music: Philip P. Bliss

And, Lord, haste the day when my
faith shall be sight,
The clouds be rolled back as a scroll,
The trump shall resound and the Lord
shall descend,
"Even so," it is well with my soul.

1. When peace, like a riv - er, at - tend - eth my way, When sor - rows like
2. Though Sa - tan should buf - fet, though tri - als should come, Let this blest as -
3. My sin— oh, the bliss of this glo - ri - ous thought: My sin— not in
4. And, Lord, haste the day when the faith shall be sight, The clouds be rolled

sea bil - lows roll; What - ev - er my lot, Thou hast taught me to say,
sur - ance con - trol, That Christ has re - gard - ed my help - less es - tate,
part, but the whole is nailed to the cross and I bear it no more,
back as a scroll, The trump shall re - sound and the Lord shall de - scend,

Chorus

"It is well, it is well with my soul." It is well with my
And hath shed His own blood for my soul. It is well
Praise the Lord, praise the Lord, O my soul!
"E - ven so," it is well with my soul.

soul, It is well, it is well with my soul.
with my soul,

By Faith

MOSES INSTITUTED THE PASSOVER

By faith he instituted the Passover
and the sprinkling of the blood, so
that the destroyer of the firstborn
might not touch the Israelites.

HEBREWS 11:28

EXODUS 12:21-28

21 Then Moses summoned all the elders of Israel and said to them, "Go, select an animal from the flock according to your families, and slaughter the Passover animal. 22 Take a cluster of hyssop, dip it in the blood that is in the basin, and brush the lintel and the two doorposts with some of the blood in the basin. None of you may go out the door of his house until morning. 23 When the LORD passes through to strike Egypt and sees the blood on the lintel and the two doorposts, he will pass over the door and not let the destroyer enter your houses to strike you.

24 "Keep this command permanently as a statute for you and your descendants. 25 When you enter the land that the LORD will give you as he promised, you are to observe this ceremony. 26 When your children ask you, 'What does this ceremony mean to you?' 27 you are to reply, 'It is the Passover sacrifice to the LORD, for he passed over the houses of

the Israelites in Egypt when he struck the Egyptians, and he spared our homes.'" So the people knelt low and worshiped. [28] Then the Israelites went and did this; they did just as the LORD had commanded Moses and Aaron.

◗ GOING DEEPER

PSALM 91

THE PROTECTION OF THE MOST HIGH

[1] The one who lives under the protection of the Most High
dwells in the shadow of the Almighty.

[2] I will say concerning the LORD, who is my refuge and my fortress,
my God in whom I trust:
[3] He himself will rescue you from the bird trap,
from the destructive plague.
[4] He will cover you with his feathers;
you will take refuge under his wings.
His faithfulness will be a protective shield.
[5] You will not fear the terror of the night,
the arrow that flies by day,
[6] the plague that stalks in darkness,
or the pestilence that ravages at noon.
[7] Though a thousand fall at your side
and ten thousand at your right hand,
the pestilence will not reach you.
[8] You will only see it with your eyes
and witness the punishment of the wicked.

[9] Because you have made the LORD—my refuge,
the Most High—your dwelling place,
[10] no harm will come to you;
no plague will come near your tent.
[11] For he will give his angels orders concerning you,
to protect you in all your ways.
[12] They will support you with their hands
so that you will not strike your foot against a stone.

¹³ You will tread on the lion and the cobra;
you will trample the young lion and the serpent.

¹⁴ Because he has his heart set on me,
I will deliver him;
I will protect him because he knows my name.
¹⁵ When he calls out to me, I will answer him;
I will be with him in trouble.
I will rescue him and give him honor.
¹⁶ I will satisfy him with a long life
and show him my salvation.

1 PETER 1:18-21

¹⁸ For you know that you were redeemed from your empty way of life inherited from your ancestors, not with perishable things like silver or gold, ¹⁹ but with the precious blood of Christ, like that of an unblemished and spotless lamb. ²⁰ He was foreknown before the foundation of the world but was revealed in these last times for you. ²¹ Through him you believe in God, who raised him from the dead and gave him glory, so that your faith and hope are in God.

REVELATION 12:10-11

¹⁰ Then I heard a loud voice in heaven say,

The salvation and the power
and the kingdom of our God
and the authority of his Christ
have now come,
because the accuser of our brothers and sisters,
who accuses them
before our God day and night,
has been thrown down.
¹¹ They conquered him
by the blood of the Lamb
and by the word of their testimony;
for they did not love their lives
to the point of death.

———

By Faith

THEY CROSSED

By faith they crossed the Red Sea
as though they were on dry land.
When the Egyptians attempted to
do this, they were drowned.

HEBREWS 11:29

THE EGYPTIAN PURSUIT

[5] When the king of Egypt was told that the people had fled, Pharaoh and his officials changed their minds about the people and said, "What have we done? We have released Israel from serving us." [6] So he got his chariot ready and took his troops with him; [7] he took six hundred of the best chariots and all the rest of the chariots of Egypt, with officers in each one. [8] The LORD hardened the heart of Pharaoh king of Egypt, and he pursued the Israelites, who were going out defiantly. [9] The Egyptians—all Pharaoh's horses and chariots, his horsemen, and his army—chased after them and caught up with them as they camped by the sea beside Pi-hahiroth, in front of Baal-zephon.

[10] As Pharaoh approached, the Israelites looked up and there were the Egyptians coming after them! The Israelites were terrified and cried out to the LORD for help. [11] They said to Moses, "Is it because there are no graves in Egypt that you have taken us away to die in the wilderness? What have you done to us by bringing us out of Egypt? [12] Isn't this what we told you in Egypt: Leave us alone so that we may serve the Egyptians? It would have been better for us to serve the Egyptians than to die in the wilderness."

[13] But Moses said to the people, "Don't be afraid. Stand firm and see the LORD's salvation that he will accomplish for you today; for the Egyptians you see today, you will never see again. [14] The LORD will fight for you, and you must be quiet."

ESCAPE THROUGH THE RED SEA

[15] The LORD said to Moses, "Why are you crying out to me? Tell the Israelites to break camp.

[16] As for you, lift up your staff, stretch out your hand over the sea, and divide it so that the Israelites can go through the sea on dry ground. [17] As for me, I am going to harden the hearts of the Egyptians so that they will go in after them, and I will receive glory by means of Pharaoh, all his army, and his chariots and horsemen. [18] The Egyptians will know that I am the LORD when I receive glory through Pharaoh, his chariots, and his horsemen."

[19] Then the angel of God, who was going in front of the Israelite forces, moved and went behind them. The pillar of cloud moved from in front of them and stood behind them. [20] It came between the Egyptian and Israelite forces. There was cloud and darkness, it lit up the night, and neither group came near the other all night long.

[21] Then Moses stretched out his hand over the sea. The LORD drove the sea back with a powerful east wind all that night and turned the sea into dry land. So the waters were divided, [22] and the Israelites went through the sea on dry ground, with the waters like a wall to them on their right and their left.

[23] The Egyptians set out in pursuit—all Pharaoh's horses, his chariots, and his horsemen—and went into the sea after them. [24] During the morning watch, the LORD looked down at the Egyptian forces from the pillar of fire and cloud, and threw the Egyptian forces into confusion. [25] He caused their chariot wheels to swerve and made them drive with difficulty. "Let's get away from Israel," the Egyptians said, "because the LORD is fighting for them against Egypt!"

²⁶ Then the LORD said to Moses, "Stretch out your hand over the sea so that the water may come back on the Egyptians, on their chariots and horsemen." ²⁷ So Moses stretched out his hand over the sea, and at daybreak the sea returned to its normal depth. While the Egyptians were trying to escape from it, the LORD threw them into the sea. ²⁸ The water came back and covered the chariots and horsemen, plus the entire army of Pharaoh that had gone after them into the sea. Not even one of them survived.

²⁹ But the Israelites had walked through the sea on dry ground, with the waters like a wall to them on their right and their left. ³⁰ That day the LORD saved Israel from the power of the Egyptians, and Israel saw the Egyptians dead on the seashore. ³¹ When Israel saw the great power that the LORD used against the Egyptians, the people feared the LORD and believed in him and in his servant Moses.

EXODUS 15:1–21

ISRAEL'S SONG

¹ Then Moses and the Israelites sang this song to the LORD. They said:

I will sing to the LORD,
for he is highly exalted;
he has thrown the horse
and its rider into the sea.
² The LORD is my strength and my song;
he has become my salvation.
This is my God, and I will praise him,
my father's God, and I will exalt him.
³ The LORD is a warrior;
the LORD is his name.

⁴ He threw Pharaoh's chariots
and his army into the sea;
the elite of his officers
were drowned in the Red Sea.
⁵ The floods covered them;
they sank to the depths like a stone.
⁶ LORD, your right hand is glorious in power.
LORD, your right hand shattered the enemy.
⁷ You overthrew your adversaries

by your great majesty.
You unleashed your burning wrath;
it consumed them like stubble.
⁸ The water heaped up at the blast from your nostrils;
the currents stood firm like a dam.
The watery depths congealed in the heart of the sea.
⁹ The enemy said:
"I will pursue, I will overtake,
I will divide the spoil.
My desire will be gratified at their expense.
I will draw my sword;
my hand will destroy them."
¹⁰ But you blew with your breath,
and the sea covered them.
They sank like lead
in the mighty waters.

¹¹ LORD, who is like you among the gods?
Who is like you, glorious in holiness,
revered with praises, performing wonders?
¹² You stretched out your right hand,
and the earth swallowed them.
¹³ With your faithful love,
you will lead the people
you have redeemed;
you will guide them to your holy dwelling
with your strength.

¹⁴ When the peoples hear, they will shudder;
anguish will seize the inhabitants of Philistia.
¹⁵ Then the chiefs of Edom will be terrified;
trembling will seize the leaders of Moab;
all the inhabitants of Canaan will panic;
¹⁶ terror and dread will fall on them.
They will be as still as a stone
because of your powerful arm
until your people pass by, LORD,
until the people whom you purchased pass by.

¹⁷ You will bring them in and plant them
on the mountain of your possession;

Lord, you have prepared the place
for your dwelling;
Lord, your hands have established the sanctuary.
¹⁸ The Lord will reign forever and ever!

¹⁹ When Pharaoh's horses with his chariots and horsemen went into the sea, the Lord brought the water of the sea back over them. But the Israelites walked through the sea on dry ground. ²⁰ Then the prophetess Miriam, Aaron's sister, took a tambourine in her hand, and all the women came out following her with tambourines and dancing. ²¹ Miriam sang to them:

Sing to the Lord,
for he is highly exalted;
he has thrown the horse
and its rider into the sea.

◆ GOING DEEPER

ISAIAH 43:1-4

RESTORATION OF ISRAEL

¹ Now this is what the Lord says—
the one who created you, Jacob,
and the one who formed you, Israel—
"Do not fear, for I have redeemed you;
I have called you by your name; you are mine.
² When you pass through the waters,
I will be with you,
and the rivers will not overwhelm you.
When you walk through the fire,
you will not be scorched,
and the flame will not burn you.
³ For I am the Lord your God,
the Holy One of Israel, and your Savior.
I have given Egypt as a ransom for you,
Cush and Seba in your place.
⁴ Because you are precious in my sight
and honored, and I love you,
I will give people in exchange for you
and nations instead of your life."

By Faith

THE WALLS FELL

———

By faith the walls of
Jericho fell down after
being marched around
by the Israelites for
seven days.

HEBREWS 11:30

DAY   26

¹ After the death of Moses the Lord's servant, the Lord spoke to Joshua son of Nun, Moses's assistant: ² "Moses my servant is dead. Now you and all the people prepare to cross over the Jordan to the land I am giving the Israelites. ³ I have given you every place where the sole of your foot treads, just as I promised Moses. ⁴ Your territory will be from the wilderness and Lebanon to the great river, the Euphrates River—all the land of the Hittites—and west to the Mediterranean Sea. ⁵ No one will be able to stand against you as long as you live. I will be with you, just as I was with Moses. I will not leave you or abandon you.

⁶ "Be strong and courageous, for you will distribute the land I swore to their ancestors to give them as an inheritance. ⁷ Above all, be strong and very courageous to observe carefully the whole instruction my servant Moses commanded you. Do not turn from it to the right or the left, so that you will have success wherever you go. ⁸ This book of instruction must not depart from your mouth; you are to meditate on it day and night so that you may carefully observe everything written in it. For then you will prosper and succeed in whatever you do. ⁹ Haven't I commanded you: be strong and courageous? Do not be afraid or discouraged, for the Lord your God is with you wherever you go."

JOSHUA 6:1-21

THE CONQUEST OF JERICHO

¹ Now Jericho was strongly fortified because of the Israelites—no one leaving or entering. ² The Lord said to Joshua, "Look, I have handed Jericho, its king, and its best soldiers over to you. ³ March around the city with all the men of war, circling the city one time. Do this for six days. ⁴ Have seven priests carry seven ram's-horn trumpets in front of the ark. But on the seventh day, march around the city seven times, while the priests blow the rams' horns. ⁵ When there is a prolonged blast of the horn and you hear its sound, have all the troops give a mighty shout. Then the city wall will collapse, and the troops will advance, each man straight ahead."

⁶ So Joshua son of Nun summoned the priests and said to them, "Take up the ark of the covenant and have seven priests carry seven rams' horns in front of the ark of the Lord." ⁷ He said to the troops, "Move forward, march around the city, and have the armed men go ahead of the ark of the Lord."

8 After Joshua had spoken to the troops, seven priests carrying seven rams' horns before the LORD moved forward and blew the rams' horns; the ark of the LORD's covenant followed them. 9 While the rams' horns were blowing, the armed men went in front of the priests who blew the rams' horns, and the rear guard went behind the ark. 10 But Joshua had commanded the troops, "Do not shout or let your voice be heard. Don't let one word come out of your mouth until the time I say, 'Shout!' Then you are to shout." 11 So the ark of the LORD was carried around the city, circling it once. They returned to the camp and spent the night there.

12 Joshua got up early the next morning. The priests took the ark of the LORD, 13 and the seven priests carrying seven rams' horns marched in front of the ark of the LORD. While the rams' horns were blowing, the armed men went in front of them, and the rear guard went behind the ark of the LORD. 14 On the second day they marched around the city once and returned to the camp. They did this for six days.

15 Early on the seventh day, they started at dawn and marched around the city seven times in the same way. That was the only day they marched around the city seven times. 16 After the seventh time, the priests blew the rams' horns, and Joshua said to the troops, "Shout! For the LORD has given you the city. 17 But the city and everything in it are set apart to the LORD for destruction. Only Rahab the prostitute and everyone with her in the house will live, because she hid the messengers we sent. 18 But keep yourselves from the things set apart, or you will be set apart for destruction. If you take any of those things, you will set apart the camp of Israel for destruction and make trouble for it. 19 For all the silver and gold, and the articles of bronze and iron, are dedicated to the LORD and must go into the LORD's treasury."

20 So the troops shouted, and the rams' horns sounded. When they heard the blast of the ram's horn, the troops gave a great shout, and the wall collapsed. The troops advanced into the city, each man straight ahead, and they captured the city. 21 They completely destroyed everything in the city with the sword—every man and woman, both young and old, and every ox, sheep, and donkey.

⛉ GOING DEEPER

PSALM 98:1-3

PRAISE THE KING

A psalm.

1 Sing a new song to the LORD,
for he has performed wonders;
his right hand and holy arm
have won him victory.
2 The LORD has made his victory known;
he has revealed his righteousness
in the sight of the nations.
3 He has remembered his love
and faithfulness to the house of Israel;
all the ends of the earth
have seen our God's victory.

04

WEEKLY RESPONSE

Review any notes you took throughout your reading this week. Use them as you answer the following questions, reflecting on how these stories encourage you to respond to God in faith in your own life.

What aspects of God's character stood out to you, challenged you, or encouraged you?

How did the people in this week's stories respond to God?

What surprised you
about their stories?

What parts of their
experiences made it
difficult for them
to respond to God
in faith?

How have you seen God
working in your own
life this week? What
might it look like for
you to respond to Him
in faith?

GRACE DAY

Take this day to catch up on your reading,
pray, and rest in the presence of the Lord.

Through him you believe
in God, who raised him
from the dead and gave him
glory, so that your faith
and hope are in God.

1 PETER 1:21

WEEKLY DAY ————————

Scripture is God-breathed and true. When we memorize it, we carry the good news of Jesus with us wherever we go.

For this plan, we are memorizing Hebrews 5:7–9, a passage from this study that summarizes how Jesus is both the firm foundation of our faith and how we are to imitate Jesus's faith in our own response to God. This week, memorize verse 9.

SEE TIPS FOR MEMORIZING SCRIPTURE ON PAGE 164.

TRUTH

7 During his earthly life, he offered prayers and appeals with loud cries and tears to the one who was able to save him from death, and he was heard because of his reverence. 8 Although he was the Son, he learned obedience from what he suffered. 9 After he was perfected, he became the source of eternal salvation for all who obey him...

By Faith

RAHAB WELCOMED

By faith Rahab the prostitute
welcomed the spies in peace
and didn't perish with those
who disobeyed.

HEBREWS 11:31

JOSHUA 2

SPIES SENT TO JERICHO

¹ Joshua son of Nun secretly sent two men as spies from the Acacia Grove, saying, "Go and scout the land, especially Jericho." So they left, and they came to the house of a prostitute named Rahab, and stayed there.

² The king of Jericho was told, "Look, some of the Israelite men have come here tonight to investigate the land." ³ Then the king of Jericho sent word to Rahab and said, "Bring out the men who came to you and entered your house, for they came to investigate the entire land."

⁴ But the woman had taken the two men and hidden them. So she said, "Yes, the men did come to me, but I didn't know where they were from. ⁵ At nightfall, when the city gate was about to close, the men went out, and I don't know where they were going. Chase after them quickly, and you can catch up with them!" ⁶ But she had taken them up to the roof and hidden them among the stalks of flax that she had arranged on the roof. ⁷ The men pursued them along the road to the fords of the Jordan, and as soon as they left to pursue them, the city gate was shut.

THE PROMISE TO RAHAB

⁸ Before the men fell asleep, she went up on the roof ⁹ and said to them, "I know that the LORD has given you this land and that the terror of you has fallen on us, and everyone who lives in the land is panicking because of you. ¹⁰ For we have heard how the LORD dried up the water of the Red Sea before you when you came out of Egypt, and what you did to Sihon and Og, the two Amorite kings you completely destroyed across the Jordan. ¹¹ When we heard this, we lost heart, and everyone's courage failed because of you,

for the LORD your God is God in heaven above and on earth below.

¹² Now please swear to me by the LORD that you will also show kindness to my father's family, because I showed kindness to you. Give me a sure sign ¹³ that you will spare the lives of my father, mother, brothers, sisters, and all who belong to them, and save us from death."

¹⁴ The men answered her, "We will give our lives for yours. If you don't report our mission, we will show kindness and faithfulness to you when the LORD gives us the land."

¹⁵ Then she let them down by a rope through the window, since she lived in a house that was built into the wall of the city. ¹⁶ "Go to the hill country so that the men pursuing you won't find you," she said to them. "Hide there for three days until they return; afterward, go on your way."

¹⁷ The men said to her, "We will be free from this oath you made us swear, ¹⁸ unless, when we enter the land, you tie this scarlet cord to the window through which you let us down. Bring your father, mother, brothers, and all your father's family into your house. ¹⁹ If anyone goes out the doors of your house, his death will be his own fault, and we will be innocent. But if anyone with you in the house should be harmed, his death will be our fault. ²⁰ And if you report our mission, we are free from the oath you made us swear."

²¹ "Let it be as you say," she replied, and she sent them away. After they had gone, she tied the scarlet cord to the window.

²² So the two men went into the hill country and stayed there three days until the pursuers had returned. They searched all along the way, but did not find them. ²³ Then the men returned, came down from the hill country, and crossed the Jordan. They went to Joshua son of Nun and reported everything that had happened to them. ²⁴ They told Joshua, "The LORD has handed over the entire land to us. Everyone who lives in the land is also panicking because of us."

JOSHUA 6:22–25

RAHAB AND HER FAMILY SPARED

²² Joshua said to the two men who had scouted the land, "Go to the prostitute's house and bring the woman out of there, and all who are with her, just as you swore to her." ²³ So the young men who had scouted went in and brought out Rahab and her father, mother, brothers, and all who belonged to her. They brought out her whole family and settled them outside the camp of Israel.

²⁴ They burned the city and everything in it, but they put the silver and gold and the articles of bronze and iron into the treasury of the LORD's house. ²⁵ However, Joshua spared Rahab the prostitute, her father's family, and all who belonged to her, because she hid the messengers Joshua had sent to spy on Jericho, and she still lives in Israel today.

PROVERBS 16:7

When a person's ways please the LORD,
he makes even his enemies to be at peace with him.

MATTHEW 10:40-42

A CUP OF COLD WATER

40 "The one who welcomes you welcomes me, and the one who welcomes me welcomes him who sent me. 41 Anyone who welcomes a prophet because he is a prophet will receive a prophet's reward. And anyone who welcomes a righteous person because he's righteous will receive a righteous person's reward. 42 And whoever gives even a cup of cold water to one of these little ones because he is a disciple, truly I tell you, he will never lose his reward."

JAMES 2:24-26

24 You see that a person is justified by works and not by faith alone. 25 In the same way, wasn't Rahab the prostitute also justified by works in receiving the messengers and sending them out by a different route? 26 For just as the body without the spirit is dead, so also faith without works is dead.

Many Saw

GOD
MOVE

DAY 30

———

And what more can I say?
Time is too short for me to
tell about Gideon, Barak,
Samson, Jephthah, David,
Samuel, and the prophets,
who by faith conquered
kingdoms, administered
justice, obtained promises,
shut the mouths of lions,
quenched the raging of
fire, escaped the edge of
the sword, gained strength
in weakness, became mighty
in battle, and put foreign
armies to flight.

HEBREWS 11:32–34

♥ GOING DEEPER

PSALM 44:1–8

ISRAEL'S COMPLAINT

For the choir director. A Maskil *of the sons of Korah.*

1 God, we have heard with our ears—
our ancestors have told us—
the work you accomplished in their days,
in days long ago:
2 In order to plant them,
you displaced the nations by your hand;
in order to settle them,
you brought disaster on the peoples.
3 For they did not take the land by
    their sword—
their arm did not bring them victory—
but by your right hand, your arm,
and the light of your face,
because you were favorable toward them.

The People of
Hebrews 11

In Hebrews 11, eighteen specific people are highlighted—and other judges, prophets, and kings called out more generally—for how they lived out their faith. Having read through the stories of these men and women, you might be asking questions like, "Why these people?" "Why not others?"

Scripture is full of people who lived and acted in faith. While this chapter highlights several key people in biblical history, it is by no means comprehensive. It also does not mean that those listed here were perfect—people in Scripture rarely fall into neat categories of "good" and "bad."

While we might be tempted to put some on a pedestal and pass judgment on others, their inclusion in this chapter does not mean they were inherently better. They were simply imperfect people open to being used by a perfect, holy God. These examples of faith in God in the middle of various trials and suffering provide the reminder that it is possible to endure great hardship for the sake of an even greater hope.

Because this compilation of names and stories is full of broken yet faithful people, we too can confidently move through our own suffering in faith, taking our place alongside this great cloud of witnesses because of the perfect work of Jesus.

⁴ You are my King, my God,
who ordains victories for Jacob.
⁵ Through you we drive back our foes;
through your name we trample our enemies.
⁶ For I do not trust in my bow,
and my sword does not bring me victory.
⁷ But you give us victory over our foes
and let those who hate us be disgraced.
⁸ We boast in God all day long;
we will praise your name forever.   *Selah*

ISAIAH 9:2-7

² The people walking in darkness
have seen a great light;
a light has dawned
on those living in the land of darkness.
³ You have enlarged the nation
and increased its joy.
The people have rejoiced before you
as they rejoice at harvest time
and as they rejoice when dividing spoils.
⁴ For you have shattered their oppressive yoke
and the rod on their shoulders,
the staff of their oppressor,
just as you did on the day of Midian.
⁵ For every trampling boot of battle
and the bloodied garments of war
will be burned as fuel for the fire.
⁶ For a child will be born for us,
a son will be given to us,
and the government will be on his shoulders.
He will be named
Wonderful Counselor, Mighty God,
Eternal Father, Prince of Peace.
⁷ The dominion will be vast,
and its prosperity will never end.
He will reign on the throne of David
and over his kingdom,
to establish and sustain it
with justice and righteousness from now on and forever.
The zeal of the Lord of Armies will accomplish this.

MARY'S PRAISE

⁴⁶ And Mary said:

> My soul magnifies the Lord,
> ⁴⁷ and my spirit rejoices in God my Savior,
> ⁴⁸ because he has looked with favor
> on the humble condition of his servant.
> Surely, from now on all generations
> will call me blessed,
> ⁴⁹ because the Mighty One
> has done great things for me,
> and his name is holy.
> ⁵⁰ His mercy is from generation to generation
> on those who fear him.
> ⁵¹ He has done a mighty deed with his arm;
> he has scattered the proud
> because of the thoughts of their hearts;
> ⁵² he has toppled the mighty from their thrones
> and exalted the lowly.
> ⁵³ He has satisfied the hungry with good things
> and sent the rich away empty.
> ⁵⁴ He has helped his servant Israel,
> remembering his mercy
> ⁵⁵ to Abraham and his descendants forever,
> just as he spoke to our ancestors.

1 JOHN 1:1–3

PROLOGUE: OUR DECLARATION

¹ What was from the beginning, what we have heard, what we have seen with our eyes, what we have observed and have touched with our hands, concerning the word of life— ² that life was revealed, and we have seen it and we testify and declare to you the eternal life that was with the Father and was revealed to us— ³ what we have seen and heard we also declare to you, so that you may also have fellowship with us; and indeed our fellowship is with the Father and with his Son, Jesus Christ.

The World Was Not

WORTHY OF THEM

Women received their dead, raised
to life again. Other people were
tortured, not accepting release,
so that they might gain a better
resurrection. Others experienced
mockings and scourgings, as well as
bonds and imprisonment. They were
stoned, they were sawed in two, they
died by the sword, they wandered
about in sheepskins, in goatskins,
destitute, afflicted, and mistreated.
The world was not worthy of them.
They wandered in deserts and on
mountains, hiding in caves and holes
in the ground.

HEBREWS 11:35–38

DAY   31

ISAIAH 63:7-9

REMEMBRANCE OF GRACE

⁷ I will make known the Lord's faithful love
and the Lord's praiseworthy acts,
because of all the Lord has done for us—
even the many good things
he has done for the house of Israel,
which he did for them based on his compassion
and the abundance of his faithful love.
⁸ He said, "They are indeed my people,
children who will not be disloyal,"
and he became their Savior.
⁹ In all their suffering, he suffered,
and the angel of his presence saved them.
He redeemed them
because of his love and compassion;
he lifted them up and carried them
all the days of the past.

ROMANS 5:1-5

FAITH TRIUMPHS

¹ Therefore, since we have been justified by faith, we have peace with God through our Lord Jesus Christ. ² We have also obtained access through him by faith into this grace in which we stand, and we boast in the hope of the glory of God. ³ And not only that, but we also boast in our afflictions, because we know that affliction produces endurance, ⁴ endurance produces proven character, and proven character produces hope. ⁵ This hope will not disappoint us, because God's love has been poured out in our hearts through the Holy Spirit who was given to us.

ROMANS 8:28-39

²⁸ We know that all things work together for the good of those who love God, who are called according to his purpose. ²⁹ For those he foreknew he also predestined to be conformed to the image of his Son, so that he would be the firstborn among many brothers and sisters. ³⁰ And those he predestined, he also called; and those he called, he also justified; and those he justified, he also glorified.

[31] What, then, are we to say about these things? If God is for us, who is against us? [32] He did not even spare his own Son but gave him up for us all. How will he not also with him grant us everything? [33] Who can bring an accusation against God's elect? God is the one who justifies. [34] Who is the one who condemns? Christ Jesus is the one who died, but even more, has been raised; he also is at the right hand of God and intercedes for us. [35] Who can separate us from the love of Christ? Can affliction or distress or persecution or famine or nakedness or danger or sword? [36] As it is written:

> Because of you
> we are being put to death all day long;
> we are counted as sheep to be slaughtered.

[37] No, in all these things we are more than conquerors through him who loved us. [38] For I am persuaded that

neither death nor life, nor angels nor rulers, nor things present nor things to come, nor powers, [39] nor height nor depth, nor any other created thing will be able to separate us from the love of God that is in Christ Jesus our Lord.

2 CORINTHIANS 1:3–7

THE GOD OF COMFORT

[3] Blessed be the God and Father of our Lord Jesus Christ, the Father of mercies and the God of all comfort. [4] He comforts us in all our affliction, so that we may be able to comfort those who are in any kind of affliction, through the comfort we ourselves receive from God. [5] For just as the sufferings of Christ overflow to us, so also through Christ our comfort overflows. [6] If we are afflicted, it is for your comfort and salvation. If we are comforted, it is for your comfort, which produces in you patient endurance of the same sufferings that we suffer. [7] And our hope for you is firm, because we know that as you share in the sufferings, so you will also share in the comfort.

God Provided

SOMETHING BETTER

All these were approved through their
faith, but they did not receive what
was promised, since God had provided
something better for us, so that they
would not be made perfect without us.

HEBREWS 11:39–40

🛡 GOING DEEPER

HEBREWS 1:1-3

THE NATURE OF THE SON

¹ Long ago God spoke to our ancestors by the prophets at different times
and in different ways. ² In these last days, he has spoken to us by his
Son. God has appointed him heir of all things and made the universe
through him. ³ The Son is the radiance of God's glory and the exact
expression of his nature, sustaining all things by his powerful word. After
making purification for sins, he sat down at the right hand of the Majesty
on high.

HEBREWS 2:9-18

⁹ But we do see Jesus—made lower than the angels for a short time so that by God's grace he might taste death for everyone—crowned with glory and honor because he suffered death.

¹⁰ For in bringing many sons and daughters to glory, it was entirely appropriate that God—for whom and through whom all things exist—should make the pioneer of their salvation perfect through sufferings. ¹¹ For the one who sanctifies and those who are sanctified all have one Father. That is why Jesus is not ashamed to call them brothers and sisters, ¹² saying:

I will proclaim your name to my brothers and sisters;
I will sing hymns to you in the congregation.

¹³ Again, I will trust in him. And again, Here I am with the children God gave me.

¹⁴ Now since the children have flesh and blood in common, Jesus also shared in these, so that through his death he might destroy the one holding the power of death—that is, the devil— ¹⁵ and free those who were held in slavery all their lives by the fear of death. ¹⁶ For it is clear that he does not reach out to help angels, but to help Abraham's offspring. ¹⁷ Therefore, he had to be like his brothers and sisters in every way, so that he could become a merciful and faithful high priest in matters pertaining to God, to make atonement for the sins of the people. ¹⁸ For since he himself has suffered when he was tempted, he is able to help those who are tempted.

1 TIMOTHY 6:11-16

FIGHT THE GOOD FIGHT

¹¹ But you, man of God, flee from these things, and pursue righteousness, godliness, faith, love, endurance, and gentleness. ¹² Fight the good fight of the faith. Take hold of eternal life to which you were called and about which you have made a good confession in the presence of many witnesses. ¹³ In the presence of God, who gives life to all, and of Christ Jesus, who gave a good confession before Pontius Pilate, I charge you ¹⁴ to keep this command without fault or failure until the appearing of

our Lord Jesus Christ. ¹⁵ God will bring this about in his own time. He is the blessed and only Sovereign, the King of kings, and the Lord of lords, ¹⁶ who alone is immortal and who lives in unapproachable light, whom no one has seen or can see, to him be honor and eternal power. Amen.

1 PETER 1:3-9

A LIVING HOPE

³ Blessed be the God and Father of our Lord Jesus Christ. Because of his great mercy he has given us new birth into a living hope through the resurrection of Jesus Christ from the dead ⁴ and into an inheritance that is imperishable, undefiled, and unfading, kept in heaven for you. ⁵ You are being guarded by God's power through faith for a salvation that is ready to be revealed in the last time. ⁶ You rejoice in this, even though now for a short time, if necessary, you suffer grief in various trials ⁷ so that the proven character of your faith—more valuable than gold which, though perishable, is refined by fire—may result in praise, glory, and honor at the revelation of Jesus Christ.

⁸ *Though you have not seen him, you love him;*
though not seeing him now, you believe in him,
and you rejoice with inexpressible and glorious joy,
⁹ *because you are receiving the goal of your faith,*
the salvation of your souls.

Live by

FAITH

On the last day of this reading plan,
read Hebrews 11 again in its entirety,
remembering these examples of men and
women who endured in faith.

DAY   3 3

HEBREWS 11

LIVING BY FAITH

¹ Now faith is the reality of what is hoped for, the proof of what is not seen. ² For by this our ancestors were approved.

³ By faith we understand that the universe was created by the word of God, so that what is seen was made from things that are not visible.

⁴ By faith Abel offered to God a better sacrifice than Cain did. By faith he was approved as a righteous man, because God approved his gifts, and even though he is dead, he still speaks through his faith.

⁵ By faith Enoch was taken away, and so he did not experience death. He was not to be found because God took him away. For before he was taken away, he was approved as one who pleased God. ⁶ Now without faith it is impossible to please God, since the one who draws near to him must believe that he exists and that he rewards those who seek him.

⁷ By faith Noah, after he was warned about what was not yet seen and motivated by godly fear, built an ark to deliver his family. By faith he condemned the world and became an heir of the righteousness that comes by faith.

⁸ By faith Abraham, when he was called, obeyed and set out for a place that he was going to receive as an inheritance. He went out, even though he did not know where he was going. ⁹ By faith he stayed as a foreigner in the land of promise, living in tents as did Isaac and Jacob, coheirs of the same promise. ¹⁰ For he was looking forward to the city that has foundations, whose architect and builder is God.

¹¹ By faith even Sarah herself, when she was unable to have children, received power to conceive offspring, even though she was past the age, since she considered that the one who had promised was faithful. ¹² Therefore, from one man—in fact, from one as good as

dead—came offspring as numerous as the stars of the sky and as innumerable as the grains of sand along the seashore.

[13] These all died in faith, although they had not received the things that were promised. But they saw them from a distance, greeted them, and confessed that they were foreigners and temporary residents on the earth. [14] Now those who say such things make it clear that they are seeking a homeland. [15] If they were thinking about where they came from, they would have had an opportunity to return. [16] But they now desire a better place—a heavenly one. Therefore, God is not ashamed to be called their God, for he has prepared a city for them.

[17] By faith Abraham, when he was tested, offered up Isaac. He received the promises and yet he was offering his one and only son, [18] the one to whom it had been said, Your offspring will be traced through Isaac. [19] He considered God to be able even to raise someone from the dead; therefore, he received him back, figuratively speaking.

[20] By faith Isaac blessed Jacob and Esau concerning things to come. [21] By faith Jacob, when he was dying, blessed each of the sons of Joseph, and he worshiped, leaning on the top of his staff. [22] By faith Joseph, as he was nearing the end of his life, mentioned the exodus of the Israelites and gave instructions concerning his bones.

[23] By faith Moses, after he was born, was hidden by his parents for three months, because they saw that the child was beautiful, and they didn't fear the king's edict. [24] By faith Moses, when he had grown up, refused to be called the son of Pharaoh's daughter [25] and chose to suffer with the people of God rather than to enjoy the fleeting pleasure of sin. [26] For he considered reproach for the sake of Christ to be greater wealth than the treasures of Egypt, since he was looking ahead to the reward.

[27] By faith he left Egypt behind, not being afraid of the king's anger, for Moses persevered as one who sees him who is invisible. [28] By faith he instituted the Passover and the sprinkling of the blood, so that the destroyer of the firstborn might not touch the Israelites. [29] By faith they crossed the Red Sea as though they were on dry land. When the Egyptians attempted to do this, they were drowned.

[30] By faith the walls of Jericho fell down after being marched around by the Israelites for seven days. [31] By faith Rahab the prostitute welcomed the spies in peace and didn't perish with those who disobeyed.

³² And what more can I say? Time is too short for me to tell about Gideon, Barak, Samson, Jephthah, David, Samuel, and the prophets, ³³ who by faith conquered kingdoms, administered justice, obtained promises, shut the mouths of lions, ³⁴ quenched the raging of fire, escaped the edge of the sword, gained strength in weakness, became mighty in battle, and put foreign armies to flight. ³⁵ Women received their dead, raised to life again. Other people were tortured, not accepting release, so that they might gain a better resurrection. ³⁶ Others experienced mockings and scourgings, as well as bonds and imprisonment. ³⁷ They were stoned, they were sawed in two, they died by the sword, they wandered about in sheepskins, in goatskins, destitute, afflicted, and mistreated. ³⁸ The world was not worthy of them. They wandered in deserts and on mountains, hiding in caves and holes in the ground.

³⁹ All these were approved through their faith, but they did not receive what was promised, ⁴⁰ since God had provided something better for us, so that they would not be made perfect without us.

05

WEEKLY RESPONSE

Review any notes you took throughout your reading this week. Use them as you answer the following questions, reflecting on how these stories encourage you to respond to God in faith in your own life.

What aspects of God's character stood out to you, challenged you, or encouraged you?

How did the people in this week's stories respond to God?

What surprised you
about their stories?

What parts of their
experiences made it
difficult for them
to respond to God
in faith?

How have you seen God
working in your own
life this week? What
might it look like for
you to respond to Him
in faith?

GRACE DAY

Take this day to catch up on your reading, pray, and rest in the presence of the Lord.

Fight the good fight of
the faith. Take hold of
eternal life to which you
were called and about
which you have made a good
confession in the presence
of many witnesses.

1 TIMOTHY 6:12

WEEKLY

DAY ———————————————

Scripture is God-breathed and true. When we memorize it, we carry the good news of Jesus with us wherever we go.

For this plan, we have memorized Hebrews 5:7–9, a passage from this study that summarizes how Jesus is both the firm foundation of our faith and how we are to imitate Jesus's faith in our own response to God. Now, let's memorize the whole passage together.

SEE TIPS FOR MEMORIZING SCRIPTURE ON PAGE 164.

TRUTH

HEBREWS 5:7-9

7 During his earthly life, he offered prayers and appeals with loud cries and tears to the one who was able to save him from death, and he was heard because of his reverence. 8 Although he was the Son, he learned obedience from what he suffered. 9 After he was perfected, he became the source of eternal salvation for all who obey him...

Benediction

Therefore, since we also have such a large cloud of witnesses surrounding us, let us lay aside every hindrance and the sin that so easily ensnares us. Let us run with endurance the race that lies before us, keeping our eyes on Jesus, the pioneer and perfecter of our faith. For the joy that lay before him, he endured the cross, despising the shame, and sat down at the right hand of the throne of God.

HEBREWS 12:1–2

Tips for Memorizing Scripture

At He Reads Truth, we believe Scripture memorization is an important discipline in your walk with God. Committing God's Truth to memory means He can minister to us—and we can minister to others—through His Word no matter where we are. As you approach the Weekly Truth passage in this book, try these memorization tips to see which techniques work best for you.

STUDY IT

Study the passage in its biblical context, and ask yourself a few questions before you begin to memorize it: What does this passage say? What does it mean? How would I say this in my own words? What does it teach me about God? Understanding what the passage means helps you know why it is important to carry it with you wherever you go.

Break the passage into smaller sections, memorizing a phrase at a time.

PRAY IT

Use the passage you are memorizing as a prompt for prayer.

WRITE IT

Dedicate a notebook to Scripture memorization, and write the passage over and over again.

Diagram the passage after you write it out. Place a square around the verbs, underline the nouns, and circle any adjectives or adverbs. Say the passage aloud several times, emphasizing the verbs as you repeat it. Then do the same thing again with the nouns, then the adjectives and adverbs.

Write out the first letter of each word in the passage somewhere you can reference it throughout the week as you work on your memorization.

Use a whiteboard to write out the passage. Erase a few words at a time as you continue to repeat it aloud. Keep erasing parts of the passage until you have it all committed to memory.

CREATE

If you can, make up a tune for the passage to sing as you go about your day, or try singing it to the tune of a favorite song.

Use hand signals or signs to come up with associations for each word or phrase and repeat the movements as you practice.

SAY IT

Repeat the passage out loud to yourself as you are going through the rhythm of your day—getting ready, pouring your coffee, waiting in traffic, or making dinner.

Listen to the passage read aloud to you.

Record a voice memo on your phone, and listen to it throughout the day or play it on an audio Bible.

SHARE IT

Memorize the passage with a friend, family member, or mentor. Spontaneously challenge each other to recite the passage, or pick a time to review your passage and practice saying it from memory together.

Send the passage as an encouraging text to a friend, testing yourself as you type to see how much you have memorized so far.

KEEP AT IT

Set reminders on your phone to prompt you to practice your passage.

Keep a stack of note cards with Scripture you are memorizing by your bed. Practice reciting what you've memorized previously before you go to sleep, ending with the passages you are currently learning. If you wake up in the middle of the night, review them again instead of grabbing your phone. Read them out loud before you get out of bed in the morning.

CSB BOOK ABBREVIATIONS

OLD TESTAMENT

GN Genesis

EX Exodus

LV Leviticus

NM Numbers

DT Deuteronomy

JOS Joshua

JDG Judges

RU Ruth

1SM 1 Samuel

2SM 2 Samuel

1KG 1 Kings

2KG 2 Kings

1CH 1 Chronicles

2CH 2 Chronicles

EZR Ezra

NEH Nehemiah

EST Esther

JB Job

PS Psalms

PR Proverbs

EC Ecclesiastes

SG Song of Solomon

IS Isaiah

JR Jeremiah

LM Lamentations

EZK Ezekiel

DN Daniel

HS Hosea

JL Joel

AM Amos

OB Obadiah

JNH Jonah

MC Micah

NAH Nahum

HAB Habakkuk

ZPH Zephaniah

HG Haggai

ZCH Zechariah

MAL Malachi

NEW TESTAMENT

MT Matthew

MK Mark

LK Luke

JN John

AC Acts

RM Romans

1CO 1 Corinthians

2CO 2 Corinthians

GL Galatians

EPH Ephesians

PHP Philippians

COL Colossians

1TH 1 Thessalonians

2TH 2 Thessalonians

1TM 1 Timothy

2TM 2 Timothy

TI Titus

PHM Philemon

HEB Hebrews

JMS James

1PT 1 Peter

2PT 2 Peter

1JN 1 John

2JN 2 John

3JN 3 John

JD Jude

RV Revelation

BIBLIOGRAPHY

Craddock, Fred B. "Hebrews 11:1–12:17" in *The New Interpreter's Bible Volume XII*, edited by Leander E. Keck, et al. 129–147. Nashville: Abingdon Press, 1998.

Green, E. M. B. "Persecution," in *New Bible Dictionary*, edited by D. R. W. Wood et al. Downers Grove: InterVarsity Press, 1996.

Roberts, Ronald D. "Persecution," in *The Lexham Bible Dictionary*, edited by D. R. W. Wood et al. Bellingham: Lexham Press, 2016.

You just spent 35 days in the Word of God.

My favorite day of this reading plan:

One thing I learned about God:

What was God doing in my life during this study?

How did I find delight in God's Word?

What did I learn that I want to share with someone else?

A specific passage or verse that encouraged me:

A specific passage or verse that challenged and convicted me: